Though I have spent the past three decades in recovery, the Lord has used this book to deepen my spiritual growth. Dr. Richards' insights have helped me to recognize many painful judgments in my past. My sinful nature, along with my own willful, deluded thoughts, created a cycle of sin—a death-spiral of pain, drugs, acceptance into the Manson family, and murder, resulting in the destruction of innocent lives.

I doubt your heart has caused the pain that mine has. But Jesus says, "If you are angry with someone, you are subject to judgment!" We reap what we sow, no matter how small. This book dispels all excuses to judge, no matter how painful our lives become.

This book is good news! As painful judgments are placed upon the Cross, righteousness, peace, and joy in the Holy Spirit arise. Our relationships with God and others will flourish in the kingdom of love. A rich life of healing will follow, as others are blessed through walking in His presence.

—Charles "Tex" Watson
Author of *Will You Die for Me?*
Mule Creek State Prison, Ione, CA

HOW

TO

STOP

THE

PAIN

HOW
TO
STOP
THE
PAIN

DR. JAMES B. RICHARDS

WHITAKER
HOUSE

Unless otherwise indicated, all Scripture quotations are from the King James Version of the Bible.

Scripture quotations marked (NKJV) are from the *New King James Version,* © 1979, 1980, 1982 by Thomas Nelson, Inc. Used by permission. All rights reserved.

Scripture quotations marked (NIV) are from the Holy Bible, *New International Version,* © 1973, 1978, 1984 by International Bible Society. Used by permission. All rights reserved.

Scripture quotations marked (NLT) are from the *New Living Translation,* © 1996 by Tyndale Charitable Trust. Used by permission. All rights reserved.

Scripture quotations marked (TLB) are from *The Living Bible,* © 1971 by Tyndale House Publishers. Used by permission. All rights reserved.

Scripture quotations marked (RSV) are from the *Revised Standard Version Common Bible* © 1973 by Division of Christian Education of the National Council of the Churches of Christ in the United States of America. Used by permission.

Scripture quotations marked (AMP) are from the *Amplified Bible,* Expanded Edition, © 1987 by the Zondervan Corporation and the Lockman Foundation. Used by permission.

Scripture quotations marked (MESSAGE) are from *The Message: New Testament,* © 1993 by Eugene H. Peterson. Used by permission.

Editorial note: Even at the cost of violating grammatical rules, we have chosen not to capitalize the name satan and related names.

HOW TO STOP THE PAIN

Impact Ministries
3300 N. Broad Place
Huntsville, AL 35805
www.impactministries.com

ISBN: 0-88368-722-4
Printed in the United States of America
© 2001 by James B. Richards

Whitaker House
30 Hunt Valley Circle
New Kensington, PA 15068

Library of Congress Cataloging-in-Publication Data

Richards, James B. (James Burton), 1951–
    How to stop the pain : pain is inevitable, suffering is optional / by James B. Richards.
        p. cm.
Includes bibliographical references.
    ISBN 0-88368-722-4 (pbk. : alk. paper)
    1. Judgment—Religious aspects—Christianity. 2. Suffering—Religious aspects—
Christianity. I. Title.
    BV4597.54 .R53 2001
    248.8'6—dc21   2001006065

3 4 5 6 7 8 9 10 11 12 13 14 / 11 10 09 08 07 06 05 04 03

This book is dedicated to the memory of Julie Vaughn and the family and friends who loved her till the end...

About Impact Ministries

James B. Richards is president of Impact Ministries. This multifaceted, worldwide organization is pioneering an unstoppable ministry movement that is making an impact on the entire world. Impact Ministries is committed to providing relevant, meaningful ministry to all nations, while equipping a new breed of leaders who are prepared to meet the challenges of the new millennium. To meet this worldwide demand, the ministry consists of:

1. Impact of Huntsville, a vibrant, cutting-edge, local church based in Huntsville, Alabama
2. Impact International Ministries, the missions arm of the organization that reaches the nations of the world
3. Impact International Fellowship of Ministers, a worldwide ministry base that trains, equips, and serves ministers to live their call while pioneering a new level of leadership
4. Impact International Publications, changing the way the world sees God through books, audio, video, and other published materials
5. Impact Ministries, which conducts life-changing seminars and outreaches in North America
6. Impact International School of Ministry, which provides one of the most unique ministry training opportunities in the world

For information on these and other services provided by Dr. Richards and his ministry team contact us at:

3300 N. Broad Place
Huntsville, AL 35805
256-536-9402
www.impactministries.com

Other Books by James B. Richards

Contents

❦

Introduction

-ᴥᵍᴥ-

Pain is inevitable. Suffering is optional.

The world is full of hurting people. The need to free ourselves from the incredible pains inflicted by life is escalating to desperate proportions. Society abounds with the evidence—the increase in substance abuse, the quest for spiritual enlightenment, the ever-growing industry of prescription drugs, violence at home and in schools, and the increasing inability to establish meaningful relationships.

We are living in the day regarding which the Bible says, *"And because iniquity shall abound, the love of many shall wax cold"* (Matthew 24:12). As mankind treats one another in destructive, self-centered ways, we create emotional wounds that make people afraid to love and trust. And the less we feel loved, the more pain we inflict upon each other. Thus the ever-growing cycle continues on, and pain abounds.

Most people have never acquired the tools necessary for resolving personal hurt. As a result, hurt grows into bitterness, sorrow, depression, and eventual loss of physical health. Our future becomes controlled by a past that has locked us into an unending cycle of more hurt and disappointment.

Various cults, governments, and idealistic religious leaders vainly offer us a utopian promise of a place where we can avoid

11

pain by forcing society to follow the right rules. Drugs and pop psychology offer us an escapism mentality that is little more than denial. Militant groups have tried to persuade us that violence can stop violence. Sadly, even the church offers only a victim's mentality that has us forgiving and re-forgiving our offenders, yet never finding true freedom from the pain.

One of the things in life over which we have no control is the constant barrage of offenses. Jesus Himself said, *"It is impossible but that offences come"* (Luke 17:1). If *He* said there was no way around it, trust me, there is no way around it. We have no control over the fact that pain will come. But we do have complete control over that pain's ability to turn into suffering. We can end the cycle of hurt with incredible ease. We can avoid bitterness and the need for vengeance. We can free ourselves from the pain of the past. We can even change our future.

A murder trial may drag on and on as it goes through the judicial process. Each of the victim's family members relives the horrible crime every time the case is presented. Appeal after appeal seems to make the pain of the survivors grow more intense. Often those family members stand before a news camera and announce, "If I can see the offender pay the price for his crime, I will find closure." For some reason we believe that the suffering of another individual will somehow stop our suffering. But it never really works that way. No matter how great the price the offender pays, it has no real bearing on the pain of the offended.

In Scripture, Jesus does not say very much about the person who offends us. Instead, He emphasizes that we are to "watch out" when offenses come. When offenses come, we are at far more risk than the person who committed the offense. It is true that the offender's crime is clear and blatant; it is often hard to justify. But it is easy for us to justify all manner of self-destructive behavior simply by the fact that we have been offended. Nevertheless, even though we are victims, we are still subject to the same life principles. The rules for peace and happiness do not change simply because we can now justify unacceptable behavior.

Vengeance, however, is powerful and deceptive. In fact, it is so powerful that God said He was the only One with the right to use it. *"Dearly beloved, avenge not yourselves, but rather give place unto wrath: for it is written, Vengeance is mine; I will repay, saith the Lord"* (Romans 12:19). Vengeance is punishment and retaliation. The determination to punish belongs solely to the One who has the right to judge. Judgment belongs to God.

Do you want to be free from pain and suffering? Let this book take you on a journey—a journey toward freedom from pain. The first step on this journey requires that you surrender the "right" to judge. Although this will be one of the most challenging steps you will ever take, it also will be one of the most rewarding.

I have put the principles discussed in this book into practice for more than twenty years. They have saved me from pain and bitterness countless times. Thousands have been helped by these same principles. You now hold in your hands the tools you need to free yourself from the pain of the past and to avoid suffering in the future.

One

Critical Factors

❖

*The most important thing in life is to decide what is
most important.*

—*Ken Blanchard*

ow true that is. Every moment of every day we give our time and energy to something. The question is, do we give our time to what is really important? Think about it. Will the places you put your attention and efforts today take you closer to, or farther away from, your dreams? Will the decisions you make create more confusion and pain, or less? Will the way you implement God's Word bring you more confidence in God, or less? In his book *First Things First Every Day,* Stephen Covey points out that effective time management is not about putting more activity into the same amount of time, but about doing what is important in the time you have. He calls it managing by the compass instead of the clock.* I call it *living in priority.*

Nearly all the top business trainers observe the 80/20 rule. This rule says that 20 percent of your effort will produce 80 percent of your results. The wise manager discovers the 20 percent

---

* Covey, Stephen; A. Roger Merrill; and Rebecca Merrill. *First Things First Every Day.* New York: Simon & Schuster, 1997, 19–20.

that is important, focuses his or her efforts in this critical area, and accomplishes 80 percent of the work.

Conversely, there are those who work harder and longer but do not see the same kind of productivity in life. As a result, they feel that life is unfair, and sometimes they feel like victims.

The Only Path to Happiness Is through the Son

It is easy to feel that there is a set of unwritten laws that no one ever taught you. It is easy to look at those who excel at life and feel that they are somehow more privileged than you are. You might even assume that God blessed them more than He did you. Your only options seem to be to give up or to start a mystical quest for the magic formula that will bring what you desire in life.

In daily life, as well as in business, people experience pain and failure while trying very hard to be happy. For some, this begins their mystical search to please God and somehow obtain the blessings that are described in His Word. Their journey is one of legalism, dead works, self-absorption, and frustration. You see, there is not a single thing we can do to get God to violate or deny the finished work of Jesus. The Scriptures are quite clear that we have everything that pertains to life and godliness *through Jesus.* (See 2 Peter 1:3.)

In order for God to even *consider* blessing us as a result of our efforts, He would have to completely deny the finished work of His Son. Looking for ways to earn or obtain blessings always causes us to look someplace other than the Lord Jesus and His finished work. The starting place for the pathway out of pain and into sanity is to always remind ourselves of the truth: We are accepted in Jesus. We are righteous through Him. We are free from every curse of the law because we are in Him. We are qualified for every aspect of the inheritance through Him. And every promise God has ever made to anyone is "yes" because we are in Him (2 Corinthians 1:20).

Going to the Root of the Problem

Instead of looking for some deep, hidden, mystical answer to bring joy and peace to our lives, we should simply look to the Word of God. When we came to Jesus, our Christian walk was supposed to be a journey of becoming disciples. A disciple builds his or her life on the lessons and principles of the teacher. We are to build our lives on the teachings of the Lord Jesus. Thus the answer to our dilemma is always found in Him, His finished work, His Word, and His example.

All of God's Word is important, but like everything else in life, there are critical factors. Critical factors are truths that are so broad in scope that they affect nearly every area of our lives. There are other principles that, when applied, affect *many* areas of our lives. Then there are still other principles that, when observed, solve only one problem. The critical factors solve a wide scope of problems. When we examine the Word, we find what I call "The Critical Factors for Spiritual Life." These are the areas we should observe as top priority. They are the 20 percent that will produce 80 percent of the results in our lives. The Critical Factors for Spiritual Life are those factors in which you cannot afford to fail. They are the difference between the fruit and the root. They are the underlying principles that govern many different actions.

When we deal with a "fruit" problem, it is like trying to keep bad fruit out of our fruit tree. We spend our time going round and round the tree, attempting to pick all the bad fruit. Regardless of how hard we try to keep it off, it grows back. Sometimes it grows back before we make it all the way around the tree! It is terribly discouraging to work so hard and see so few results. It is even more discouraging when the problems grow back.

16

When we go right to the "root" problem, however, we eliminate the source that is feeding the fruit. We deal with one issue, and it makes all the bad fruit stop growing. By using this method, we participate in the 80/20 rule. We act by priority. We address the critical factors.

Use These Principles for Every Root

This book addresses *one* of the most important critical factors for life. It examines one root. Nevertheless, by applying the principles discussed in this book, you can free yourself from emotional pain and turmoil that otherwise will linger for a lifetime. For the first time, you can discover what it is like to be free from the pain of the past.

You see, emotional pain becomes our window to the world. We look at everything around us and judge it in light of our past pain. Unfortunately, gazing through this framework creates an endless cycle of new pain and a reaffirmation of our false paradigm of life. For the person in pain, the past equals the future. Life becomes a series of reoccurring pains that never seems to end.

Once we are free from pain, the world looks different, and our experience becomes different. When living in a place of peace and freedom from fear of future pain, we make new decisions and establish an entirely new basis for life. In the absence of distorted thinking, we can identify the critical factors for life. Walking with God becomes "easy and light," just as Jesus promised (Matthew 11:30).

Here is my promise to you. If you will read this book and apply these principles, you will discover more personal freedom than you have ever known. Every relationship will become more peaceful and less stressful. The amount of conflict in your life will be reduced dramatically. Most of the past pain will be eliminated from your life, and you will stop creating new pain.

Your promise, though, must be this: "However challenging I find them to be, I commit myself fully to the principles that I recognize as scripturally sound. Those of which I am unsure, I will search out to discover their soundness. I will not merely read these words and forget them; I will put them to the test of life application."

Welcome to the journey for freedom!

Two

What Is Judgment?

-⊰❧⊱-

Life is a garden that grows the seeds I plant.

The Sermon on the Mount contains some of the most dynamic personal teachings of Jesus. It is here that we find one of the most important critical factors for emotional health and happiness. *"Do not judge, or you too will be judged. For in the same way you judge others, you will be judged, and with the measure you use, it will be measured to you"* (Matthew 7:1–2 NIV).

For centuries, we have missed the meaning and scope of this simple yet powerful passage. We have interpreted these verses to say, "If I judge other people, God is going to judge me." That is not what this passage says. It says that if we judge people, people will judge us.

We Get Back More than We Give

In Luke 6:38, we find the parallel passage to Matthew's: *"Give, and it shall be given unto you; good measure, pressed down, and shaken together, and running over, shall men give into your bosom."* Traditionally this Scripture is applied only to financial giving. However, Jesus was not talking about finances in this

19

verse. He was talking about what we give to others *emotionally.* Earlier, in verses 36 and 37, He said, *"Be ye therefore merciful, as your Father also is merciful. Judge not, and ye shall not be judged: condemn not, and ye shall not be condemned: forgive, and ye shall be forgiven."* Verse 38 does not go on to say that God will heap these things on you; it says *people* will heap these things back on you.

Even though this verse could apply to financial generosity, it is more specifically talking about giving mercy, passing judgment, and expressing condemnation. What I give to others emotionally and relationally is what they give back to me. Again, this is not talking about what God gives to me as a result of my actions. This is what people give to me. In other words, people respond to me in direct accordance with the way I treat them, with one exception. When they give it back, they always give me more than I gave—*"good measure, pressed down, and shaken together, and running over, shall men give into your bosom."*

If you give kindness and love, other people will give you kindness and love—*"good measure, pressed down, and shaken together, and running over."* However, if you give judgment and criticism, others will give you judgment and criticism—*"good measure, pressed down, and shaken together, and running over."* Whatever you give, people will give back to you in a greater measure than you gave to them. Never confuse people's reaction with God's reaction.

Life is somewhat like a garden. Actually, let's consider our relationships to be the garden of our lives. Our garden grows with the seeds we plant. We all know that one seed, when planted, produces a harvest larger than itself. When we plant one, we reap many. One kernel of corn grows hundreds of kernels. This is an indisputable law of life. Having said that, what is growing in your life's garden? Too often we find our lives filled with things like criticism and rejection. We wrongly assume that we had nothing to do with how others treated us, when the truth is, they usually gave back to us a harvest of how we treated them.

The Critical Factor: Judgment

The quality of our emotional life is found in the quality of our relationships. We are social, emotional, and relationship-oriented beings. We thrive on meaningful relationships. It is one of the deepest needs we have as human beings. And even though our judgments influence those relationships more than any other factor, few people even know what it means to judge.

So, what *does* it mean to judge? Although judging has many facets, I believe we all can grasp the most basic and essential aspect, which is this: Identifying what someone did is not judgment; that is merely observation. It is when we assume to know *why* a person did what he did that we have entered into judgment.

Only God has the right to judge. He alone knows why people do what they do. We do not know, nor is it our place to judge why. In many cases, people do not even know why they do what they do. Jeremiah said, *"The heart is...desperately wicked: who can know it?"* (Jeremiah 17:9). God is the only One who can truly know the heart. When people assume to know *why,* then their reactions are not based on reality; they are based on judgment. That judgment causes confusion, pain, and loss.

I remember riding along in a car with two friends. One friend had some clothes hanging in the back of the car. I looked back and realized that her clothes were blowing out the back window. Now, I had been working, and my hands were very dirty. So out of my desire to save her clothes from ruin, I shouted, "Quick, look back there!" She didn't look back. She just looked at me with a startled expression on her face. Again I said in a loud, strong voice, "Quick, look back there!" The girl never realized

I was trying to help her salvage her clothes. Instead, she began to argue with me. "Who do you think you are, yelling at me like that?" This friend passed a judgment. Rather than hear my words, she assumed my motive. She assumed that I was yelling because I was angry about something. While she was arguing with me, her clothes blew out the window.

Her reaction to me was the product of judgment. More importantly, what she experienced emotionally also was the product of judgment. She felt rejected. She felt insulted. She felt abused. All because she assumed to know *why* I was speaking to her in a loud tone of voice. The truth was, I was attempting an act of kindness. The intensity in my voice was a reflection of the urgency of the situation. I meant it all for good, but she experienced it as bad because of her judgment.

Through this simple illustration, you can see how so much conflict emerges in life. The moment you attempt to determine *why* another is doing what he or she is doing, you have given it significance. Keep in mind that nothing has the power to hurt you until you attach significance to it. Another person's actions are only as significant to you as the judgments you pass on them. The judgment you make is based on your decision about why that person did what he did. The degree of pain or insult you experience from the actions of another is based solely on the judgment you pass. And the judgment you pass is your assumption of why he did what he did.

Passing judgment causes us to react to situations inappropriately. The combination of our judgments and unacceptable behavior then begins the cycle of sowing and reaping. People heap judgment back on us because of the judgment we have sowed into their lives. Simply giving up the right to judge would break the cycle of pain and torment while salvaging many valuable relationships.

Three

Breaking the
Power of Pain

Pain is inevitable. Suffering is optional.

Matthew 7:1 is probably one of the most misinterpreted of all Scriptures: *"Judge not, that ye be not judged."* We do not know how to make it through our daily lives without judging everybody and everything around us. We think we are walking in wisdom! We think that we are discerning and that our judgments will protect us from future pain, but nothing is further from the truth. Instead, we create a world of conflict and suffering through the very judgments we think will protect us.

It is true that some events have the power to bring momentary emotional pain. However, in order for something to become an abiding torment, we must first attach significance to it. It is this significance that takes a single event and turns it into a life of suffering.

Judgment Is the Bottom Line

It seems impossible for the majority of our pain to be the product of judgment rather than events. We are so sure that the wrongs we have suffered have imprisoned us in a life of pain. But the truth is that accepting this reality—that our judgments produce our pain—is the only way out of the maze of lifelong torment.

If the events of our lives were the source of our torment, then we would have no control over our future. We would be doomed to "coincidence." Or, what is worse, in an attempt to understand life's circumstances, we would convince ourselves that God brought or allowed these things into our lives for some purpose. Of course, subjectively determining that purpose would cause us to decide *why* God allowed it. In other words, we would have to judge God.

Nothing that happens outside of you has the power to hurt you *until you judge it.* Only when you judge something does it bear significance in your life. Let me say it another way. When people do something, you judge why they did it; you decide what their motive was. Once you determine (judge) the motive, you give that event significance, or power.

In Luke 17:1 Jesus said to His disciples, *"It is impossible but that offences will come: but woe unto him, through whom they come!"* From Scripture, we can quickly ascertain that being a disciple and following Jesus does not mean that problems will not come. The religious mind thinks that trouble comes only to those who deserve it. Not so. Jesus said trouble will come. So don't waste your time trying to figure out why; doing that puts you right back into a judgment situation.

I know people who no longer walk with God because they judged that God caused or allowed certain events to happen. In light of their judgment, they thought God had rejected them.

As a result, they began to feel rejected. Their false feelings confirmed God's "rejection" and so validated their false judgment. In the end, they grew angry with God and rejected Him.

I repeat, Jesus never said that becoming His disciple would protect us from circumstance. However, He did teach us that if we are His disciples, we can build our lives on His teaching and live above the control and devastation of circumstance. This is precisely what He was teaching in this passage in Luke 17.

Our Reaction Is the Determining Factor

Jesus did not focus very much attention on what befalls the violator. Instead, He went to great lengths to help us learn the process whereby we can protect ourselves when an offense comes. He showed us that our concern should not be about the fate of the offender, but our own.

In Luke 17:3 He continued, *"Take heed to yourselves: If thy brother trespass against thee...."* We may ask, "Why should I have to take heed? I am the victim! My offender is the one who should take heed." This is the very response He warned against.

We do not fall accidentally. We fall in response to events and circumstances. It is true, there are people out there who wrong us by deliberately attempting to make us fall. However, most offenses have nearly nothing to do with us. People are not doing things because of us; they are doing things because of who *they* are. In our haste to judge, we assume that they do what they do because of us. Actually, we are so self-centered that we think *everything* a person does is because of us. It is a shocking reality for some to discover that they are not that important to anyone!

When the opportunity for offense comes, our reaction is the determining factor. Only when we react in an unscriptural way does the offense bring pain to our lives. Jesus told us what we

25

should do when we are offended. He explained how we should not discuss it with anyone. We should not get others involved. Instead, we should rebuke the offender (*not* judge him).

A Rebuke—Not Judgment—Can Bring Healing

The word *rebuke* comes from two Greek words. One means "upon," and the other means "to fix a value or to honor." (See *Strong's Concordance,* #G1909 and #G5091.) Some translate it as "to charge strongly." It could be that rebuking is nothing more than making a person aware of the *value* of their actions. To say to a person, "I know why you did this," is not a rebuke but a judgment. All we can say in a rebuke is this: "This is what you just did, and this is the effect (value) it had on me." Nothing more, nothing less. We *cannot* attach significance. We cannot use that action to judge what kind of person she is. We can tell the person that she has done this thing often. But we cannot judge the motive, the intent. We simply say, "This is what you have done; this is how it affected me." Most people are surprised when they learn the effects of their actions.

The remainder of Luke 17:3–4 gives us what should be our motive for the rebuke: *"And if he repent, forgive him. And if he trespass against thee seven times in a day, and seven times in a day turn again to thee, saying, I repent; thou shalt forgive him."* Our goal should be to bring the offender to repentance. The goal cannot be punishment. Punishment is the penalty that we think a person deserves based on our judgment. Judgment precedes vengeance. Until we pass judgment, we have no desire for vengeance. Remember, we have no right to vengeance. God said vengeance belongs to Him alone (Romans 12:19). The mere fact that we are seeking vengeance indicates that we have already passed judgment.

In most cases, when someone learns how his or her behavior is affecting us, the reply will be, "I didn't know." Then a person gets to learn how to be more tasteful in his or her behavior. At that moment a healing can happen that sets us free from the pain of the offense. Seldom does a confrontation of this sort become aggressive—unless the offended person passes judgment.

True healing happens when everyone benefits from the event. When a person offends us, we can take it as an opportunity to experience the grace of God. We can use it to grow in love and mercy. Through it we can experience in God something that we may have never had before. The offender, too, can experience something from God through the situation that he may have never experienced. For many people, this can be the input they need in order to stop offensive behavior.

Sometimes, when we confront others, we discover that we are "too touchy." In other words, there was no reason that the action should have hurt us. The Bible teaches in 1 Corinthians 13 that love is not touchy or oversensitive. Even when the issue at hand turns out to be our problem, we can still win. We can gain insight into our beliefs and actions and have an opportunity to experience healing and freedom.

When we handle offense by using sound communication and relationship principles, we stop pain before it becomes torment. In a *scriptural* confrontation, everyone has a chance to grow. Everyone has a chance to experience healing. The cycle of pain and torment can end for everyone involved.

Four

The Power of
Significance

❧

*It is not the intensity of the pain, but the significance you attach
that determines the effect.*

Jesus warned us that others would judge us with the same
standards we use to judge them. The difference, however,
is that they will give back a lot more than we gave. Then
He went on to say, *"With what measure ye mete, it shall be measured to you again"* (Matthew 7:2). The measure, or effect, that
comes back to us through any event is based on two factors. The
first is the significance we attach to the event. The second is our
motive when we do these same things. If we measure something
by giving it value, size, and significance, then that measurement
determines its effect on us.

The effect of another person's behavior has little to do with
his or her intent. But that effect has everything to do with our
judgment, or how we measure it. People may take actions with

no ill intention, yet they can have devastating effects. There can even be actions that people intend for good, but that can create massive amounts of pain. When such events happen, we think, *They are doing this to me.* The truth is, regardless of people's intentions, we are doing it to ourselves.

It All Depends on Significance

I grew up in a rough and violent situation. I saw violence at a young age as my father physically abused my mother. At some point very early in my life, my father threatened to burn the house down with my family in it. I was around eleven years old the first time I was ever knocked out. My stepfather was beating my mother, and I stepped in to protect her. When I was eighteen years old, after being away from home for five years, I went back to spend a couple of nights and visit with my family. While I was there, my stepfather attempted to kill me in my sleep.

Sometimes, when people hear parts of my testimony, they say, "I can't imagine how you can be even close to normal." They think that those circumstances should have had a greater abiding effect on my life. Although I do have emotional issues that I have not yet fully realized, the events I have described have no real significance in my life today.

What I experienced was overt rejection, which is possibly the simplest rejection to deal with; it is open and straightforward. There are few hidden agendas and little emotional manipulation in this type of rejection.

The situation with my stepfather was simple. He hated me and wanted to drive me out of the house. I hated him, and I did not want to stay in the house with him. That is easy to understand. Before I received Jesus as my Savior, I was very bitter and filled with hate for my stepfather. I thought of murdering him. After I was saved, I released him from my judgment and freed myself from the pain. Although his actions were the cause of

29

much of the pain in my life, my judgment was the source of abiding torment.

People who come to me for counseling have experienced events that were much less dramatic, yet had a more severe influence on their lives. To be honest, in the early days of my ministry, I had no compassion for these people. In my smug self-righteousness, I thought, *Get real. You haven't been through anything compared to me.* What I offered as help for those people was probably not very helpful. Eventually I came to realize that it is not the intensity of the offense that determines the pain; rather, it is always the significance we attach that determines our pain. This being the case, one person could have an extremely intense experience with very few destructive results, while another could go through an apparently harmless experience and, because of the significance attached to it, have devastating results.

In reality, it was the subtle, manipulative rejection I experienced from my grandmother that had more lasting effects than the violence I endured from my stepfather. Covert rejection is usually more difficult to resolve than overt rejection. Covert rejection has much more emotional challenge, even though it may not be as intense as open rejection. It is even more difficult to handle when it comes from people we love and trust. Being rejected by a person we hate has relatively no effect compared with being rejected by someone we love. The action is the same, but we attach significance because we pass judgment on why he or she did it.

How Would You React?

Many times someone does something as simple as not speak to us. Perhaps someone important to us fails to compliment us. Or maybe we are not praised for an accomplishment, or a parent is overprotective. We think they're angry, that they don't love us, that they don't think we're pretty, or that we don't know how to do anything. Any one of those simple events could become life-changing based on the significance we attach. For example, when a mother is overprotective, thinking she is showing love, the child usually judges it to mean, "She thinks I am stupid." Although that judgment may be incorrect, the results are demoralizing.

Imagine how the following event could become devastating. On Sunday morning, unknown to you, the pastor had to deal with a crisis situation—one that would make the difference between life and death, heaven or hell, or a saved marriage instead of a broken one. As he rushes into the church, where the service has already begun, his mind is totally occupied with that crisis. You speak to him as he walks past. He seemingly ignores you.

Nothing negative actually happened; he simply did not speak to you. However, through your feelings of inadequacy, you begin to think about it and attach significance to it; you begin to measure it. You create a judgment. You ask yourself the "W" question: "Why didn't he speak to me?" Based on how you answer that question, your self-talk could continue like this: "I don't think he likes me. As a matter of fact, I'm not sure he ever really did like me!" You attach significance to insignificant actions, and now, based on your judgment, it is measured back to you as pain and rejection. That event now has power in your life.

At this point, the matter could easily be resolved. You could approach the pastor, describe the event—without judgment—and learn that his actions had nothing to do with you. Because he was lost in thought at the time, it would not have mattered who was standing there; he would not have noticed anyone who spoke.

Or maybe you go home angry and frustrated (perhaps after withholding your offering). Then it goes a step beyond that, as you begin to tell others what the pastor did to you. "I've been faithful and loyal to that church, and the pastor has never liked me! And on top of that, he's rude to me!"

You are really hurting now. You have real mental pain and anguish, but it is not based on what the other person did to you; it is based on the judgment you passed. *"With what measure ye mete, it shall be measured to you again"* (Matthew 7:2).

Two things begin to happen. First, the way in which you relate to people, as a whole, will be the way in which other people relate to you. Then there is a quantum leap from that to "the measure that you mete." This crosses over into the realm where it has nothing to do with how anybody else responds to you as much as how it affects you in your own heart because of the significance you attach.

Since we spend our lives judging people—relating to people based on our judgments of them—our lives are full of pain and dysfunction. We don't have meaningful relationships or communication because we are always judging the real motives behind what people say or do. And it all is based on our judgment.

All it takes to break free from this destructive cycle is to refuse to judge, to refuse to attach significance to the actions of others. When another person's actions affect you negatively, simply ask if there is a problem. Don't assume, and don't attach significance. When you can learn to observe rather than judge, you can stop the pain before it becomes suffering.

Five

Observers, Not Judges

-◆✺◆-

Through judgment, observation is distorted
and discernment lost.

If judgment belongs to God, then it is highly possible that, before the Fall, Adam did not have the capacity or the tendency to judge. We know that when Adam sinned, he gained the ability to judge good and evil for himself—something that he did not previously possess. The ability to judge was a part of satan's destructive offer. Adam ultimately trusted his own judgment over God's. Possessing the power of judgment, in addition to a fearful nature, drove him away from God.

Before the Fall, Adam trusted God and His opinion. He had no need or desire to determine good and evil for himself. Prior to the Fall, Adam was an *observer* of the world. When he wanted to know *why,* he looked to his Father and Creator. There was no need for judgment because there was no fear. When Adam fell, however, he became fearful by nature. The sin nature is at heart fearful; fear was Adam's first new emotion after becoming a sinner. His self-worth plummeted, and he no longer trusted what God said about anything. In effect, he became the god of his own world; and as god, he reserved the right to judge for himself. Judgment, however, is the main act of fear.

33

As new creations in Christ Jesus with a new nature, we should be free from fear. Our self-worth should be established in our new identity in Jesus. As disciples of the Lord Jesus, we should trust His Word. We should be free from the need to judge; we should return to the place of experiencing life as an observer, free from the need to act as a god.

Watch the Fruit and Be Wise

When speaking of false prophets, Jesus said,

> *By their fruit you will recognize them. Do people pick grapes from thornbushes, or figs from thistles? Likewise every good tree bears good fruit, but a bad tree bears bad fruit. A good tree cannot bear bad fruit, and a bad tree cannot bear good fruit.* (Matthew 7:16–18 NIV)

This principle applies to everyone across the board; we have only one way of knowing people: by their fruit.

Fruit is the only thing that is observable, and fruit is something that grows over time. It is not a single event, a mistake, or even our current actions. Our fruit is our track record. We are likely to do in the future what we have done consistently in the past. Our track record is all anyone knows about us.

Knowing our track record, however, does not give anyone the right to make a judgment about our motives in any situation. It does not justify their every criticism. A person's track record simply gives us observable, measurable data so that we can use wisdom in relating to him. It does not give us the right to treat him without love and respect. And it certainly does not mean that people cannot grow and change. It simply tells us what they have a tendency to do.

Commit to becoming an observer instead of a judge. It is easy to think that if we don't know people's motives, if we fail to judge them, then we won't know how to relate to them. But this is wrong thinking. God's Word is full of wisdom about how to relate to people, how to develop trust, whom to depend on, and whom not to depend on. But in true "god of our own world" fashion, we reject His wisdom and apply our own judgment. It all comes back to fear—our fears tend to drive us to trust our judgment rather than God's. In our attempt to protect ourselves from future pain (which we fear), we judge. But instead of freeing us from pain, it distorts our observation, and true discernment is lost. The result of judgment is always more pain.

Years ago, a young man came to me in a time of financial need. This young man had grown up in our church. He and his family were very dear to me. I had helped this young man financially in the past and strained our relationship somewhat, because he was always slow in making his payments.

I loved this young man, and I was not willing to risk our friendship through another difficult financial situation. As he told me his need, my heart went out to him. I really wanted to help him, but experience told me to find another way to help. As we talked, I helped him explore other options for getting the money. He was disappointed and offended that I did not lend him the money he needed, and he left with negative feelings. I really felt bad about not helping him, but wisdom told me it was the responsible way to handle the situation.

Justifying Your Actions Is Still Judging

I want to explain something here. So often in these types of situations we feel the need to justify saying "no." The problem is, in order to justify our action, to justify saying "no," we must pass a negative judgment about the person. *It is still judgment.* The moment we justify our "no," the discomfort usually escalates to a conflict, and we destroy a valuable relationship. Even more disconcerting, we destroy our opportunity to help the person solve the root of his or her problem.

Then there are times when we want to violate wisdom. Again, we feel the need to justify our actions, so we pass a good judgment. We come up with all kinds of good reasons why the young man didn't pay on time, for example. When we create enough good judgments to justify our actions, what usually results is a bad decision. Most people pass judgments to justify their actions. This need to judge is a reflection of both fear and low self-worth. If we choose to violate wisdom and lend money to a person with a poor track record (fruit), we should simply give (as opposed to lend) it and admit to ourselves that we will probably never get it back.

Or, in an even more complex situation, people may *ask* us to pass a judgment. Of course, they will never say, "I want you to judge me." Instead, they will give us reasons for their past actions. Eventually they will ask us to trust something that cannot be measured by observation. They will ask us to judge them as good, even though their fruit was bad. Of course, it is not wrong to help someone who probably can't be trusted. It could be an act of mercy or kindness. But when it is motivated by judgment, it is not love or kindness; it is foolishness. When people provide excuses for their poor track record, they are saying, "Let me tell you *why.* I want you to judge me as a good risk even though my entire track record is bad. I want to give you an excuse to act in my behalf."

Love does not need an excuse to act. We have love because love is the product of our relationship with God. It is His character infusing our character. It is the grace of God making us able to act in Godlike character and compassion. The moment we justify our actions by a judgment, good or bad, it is no longer love.

Eventually the young man came back and apologized for how he felt about me that night. He realized that I was helping him to be a responsible man when he didn't want to be. He admitted that he had been looking for the easy way out. Now, not everyone will come back and apologize. But, as in this situation, the opportunity will be there for a future relationship. My freedom from judgment salvaged a relationship that I deeply valued. During that second visit, this young man started establishing a new track record, one that in the future would make him more trustworthy.

Learning to observe and not judge has saved me from so much pain and conflict. It also has forced me to face my own issues. Why do I often want to say "no" and lack the strength to do it? Why do I often want to say "yes" and don't follow through? Judgment! Judgment focuses on the other person so that we can excuse our actions. When we judge, we are no longer motivated by our hearts, the wisdom of God's Word, the voice of God in our hearts, or the love of God in our hearts. Instead, we are led by our attempts to be the god of our own world. And this limits us to the wisdom of our judgments.

Being free from judgment makes it possible for you to act out of your own nature. It frees you to act for your reason instead of others' reasons. It frees you from the torment of finding fault to justify your saying "no." It frees you from the need to find excuses to justify your saying "yes." And it allows your "*yea* [to] *be yea; and your nay, nay*" (James 5:12).

It is always acceptable to say, "I would rather not," or "I am uncomfortable with this." These are the types of statements that we can make without passing a judgment. When wisdom dictates, it is often valuable to say, "My past experience with you makes me believe this will have a negative outcome, and I don't want to risk our relationship." There are many things we can do and say without passing judgment—and one of the most gracious things we can ever do is give a person the opportunity to establish a new track record.

Six

Fixing You Is Killing Me

❧❦

Finding fault is the product of fear, low self-worth, and anger.

And why worry about a speck in the eye of a brother when you have a board in your own? Should you say, "Friend, let me help you get that speck out of your eye," when you can't even see because of the board in your own? Hypocrite! First get rid of the board. Then you can see to help your brother.

—*Matthew 7:3–5 TLB*

P ain would have no opportunity in our lives if we lived in harmony with one another. As social, emotional, relationship-oriented beings, we have no greater need in our lives than that of harmonious, loving relationships. Yet relationship skills are emphasized very little in the church or the secular world. As people develop intellectually, they seem to fall further and further behind in their relational skills. Much of the emptiness in our society is the result of this tragic neglect. Money, entertainment, and technology can never replace the needs of relationship.

How to Help without "Fixing"

A major turning point in my life came when I realized I needed to live at peace with people. For many years I had misguided compassion. I cared about people and wanted to help them. But my definition of helping people was to fix them. In my misguided attempts to help, I created much pain and conflict in my life and in the lives of others. I wanted peace, but I thought love fixed people. I soon found out that peace and fixing cannot coexist.

The fixer always finds himself being misunderstood. As fixers, we have all these good intentions. After all, we're doing it for their good, right? Yet we are not valued and appreciated. Why? Jesus said, in the passage quoted at the beginning of the chapter, that our attempts to fix others would be appreciated as much as our blindly sticking our fingers in a person's eye would be. Regardless of our motive, we will simply cause pain.

Jesus warned of the temptation to focus on the problems of others. The best thing I can do for you and your problems is to take care of me and my problems. This is not a self-centered statement! You see, if I take care of me—if I develop my heart to walk in love, if I am able to bring the love of God to you in your time of trouble—then I have provided you with a great service.

The moment I come to the place where I feel I can see your faults more clearly than I can see my own, I have become a hypocrite. *Strong's Concordance* defines this word for *hypocrite* as "an actor under an assumed character; a stage-player" (#G5273). In this scenario, it seems the role we are playing is God's.

Love compels us to be vigilant and sensitive to the needs in the lives of others. But, with a subtle twist of motivation, we can become more sensitive to the fault than to the need. You see, needs are usually manifested through faults. Children say they are afraid by expressing their need. They usually manifest their

39

fears by some negative behavior. Too often we see the negative behavior and never recognize the need that is generating the behavior. Singer Dottie Rambo said of Jesus, "He looked beyond my fault and saw my need."

Our warped definitions of love and "ministry" compel us to "get the splinter out of their eye." I don't know about you, but I don't want a blind person attempting to get anything out of my eye. I am afraid that, in the process, he or she would render me blind as well! That is exactly what happens when we attempt to fix others. We create pain in their lives, and then they create pain in ours. Thus the cycle of pain and conflict is reinforced in yet another area of our lives.

It is never our job to fix anyone. It is, however, our job to facilitate an environment in which God and people can work together to heal their every pain and thereby solve their every problem. In an environment of love and acceptance, people feel safe enough to address their issues. Our attempts to fix people usually put them in a defensive mode that lessens the likelihood that even God will be able to work in their lives.

Focus on Jesus, Not Faults

How did we get into this cycle in the first place? It all comes down to what we believe about God. It is our warped concept of God that justifies our hypocritical attempts to fix people. For example, we assume that God helps us by showing us our faults. But in Jeremiah 31:34 God says, *"I will forgive their iniquity, and I will remember their sin no more."* If God remembers our sins no more, then why and how would He remind us of them?

When the Scriptures describe the work of the Holy Spirit, they say that He will convict the world of sin, righteousness, and judgment (John 16:8). In the next few verses, we discover what that means.

In regard to sin, because men do not believe in me; in regard to righteousness, because I am going to the Father, where you can see me no longer; and in regard to judgment, because the prince of this world now stands condemned. (John 16:9–11 NIV)

Not one time do the Scriptures say that He will point out our faults.

Finding fault is not a work of the Holy Spirit. It is not a spiritual gift. It is neither inspired by God nor led by God. Finding fault is the product of fear, low self-worth, and anger. It is a vain attempt to end pain by controlling and forcing others to change. It is the source of more conflict and lost love than almost any other factor. Our attempts to fix each other are killing us! The proof is obvious. Our attempts never work, but we refuse to consider the board in our own eye and continue to search for the sawdust in the eyes of others.

Even when change truly is needed, transformation doesn't happen by focusing on what is wrong. Everything we know about human behavior tells us that people are transformed into whatever holds their attention. People who are focused on their faults never escape those faults. God wants you to know that the sin problem was settled by the finished work of Jesus. He wants you to know that, through faith in that finished work, you can be empowered in God's righteousness to be who God says you are.

Our call to follow Jesus is a call to a life that is focused on Him, what He is doing, and where He is going. He should become the center of our entire lives. His love, acceptance, and stability should make us the most confident, stable people in the world. In Matthew 11:28–30 Jesus promised that if we would "yoke up with Him," we would have a life that is easy and light.

To "yoke up" requires sensitivity. It means we have to be sensitive and responsive to how Jesus is moving. If our attention is on our problems or on the problems of others, we will not be aware of how He desires to move in our lives. When He is not the focus, He is no longer the influence. At this point, we do not move with Him. Instead, we often move against Him. When we attempt to fix people, we become the main obstacle blocking God's working in their lives.

Despite all that God is doing to get us to see ourselves as new creations, made righteous by the blood of Jesus, free from fear of wrath and judgment, we insist on keeping people focused on their faults. We insist that we can fix them. When we insist on these things, we are actually asking people to give us the place in their lives that belongs only to God.

This compulsion to pull the splinter out of everyone else's eye is based on our judgment. Since we know *why* people are the way they are, we are the ones who can see clearly to fix the problem. It is that very judgment that blinds us to reality and renders us unfit to be of any help to those who are hurting and struggling. It is this very mentality that causes us to inflict pain on others and provoke them into bringing pain and retaliation into our lives.

Your life is influenced by what you focus your attention on. If you will renew your mind to the truth of what God says about you, you will not focus on the splinter in another's eye. Instead, you will be removing the board from your own! The greatest service you can give to others is to take care of yourself. When you can see things clearly from God's perspective, you will always see that loving, accepting, encouraging, and nurturing are far superior to finding fault, condemning, and fixing.

Seven

"You're the Problem, Not Me!"

If I don't blame you, where does that leave me?

The Pharisees were more than just legalists, they were also externalists. In other words, they had no concept of "living out of the heart." They had reduced a relational walk with God to over six hundred daily rules of outward observation—all of which had little or no value regarding the motive of the heart. Jesus described them thus: *"These people honor me with their lips, but their hearts are far from me. They worship me in vain; their teachings are but rules taught by men"* (Matthew 15:8–9 NIV).

Judgment is always a characteristic of externalists. Since externalists do not look and listen in their own hearts, they never experience the comfort of God's love and acceptance. They have no intimacy with God. Instead, they replace that intimacy with the false sense of security that comes from finding fault in others and thereby elevating themselves. And since they measure godliness externally, there is a constant comparing, condemning, and measuring. Externalists do not try to follow God from the heart—it is all about behavior.

One of the best ways to keep people from scrutinizing your behavior is to find fault with their behavior. Not only does it take the spotlight off you, but it also gives you control over them by creating fear and self-doubt. From this emerges the mean heart of religion.

When the Pharisees asked Jesus about the coming of the kingdom of God, He replied, *"The kingdom of God does not come with your careful observation, nor will people say, 'Here it is,' or 'There it is,' because the kingdom of God is within you"* (Luke 17:20–21 NIV). Jesus pointed them to the place they never looked: within themselves. The very idea of looking to the heart is foreign to externalists. Their entire way of life is built on measuring and criticizing one another's faults.

Matthew 7:3 says, *"Why do you look at the speck of sawdust in your brother's eye and pay no attention to the plank in your own eye?"* (NIV). Judgment is a tremendous defense mechanism. Those who live in judgment always keep their focus on others in order to avoid dealing with their own issues.

In the name of ministry, we have made it an accepted agenda to fix others. This move violates every scriptural principle concerning the work of the Holy Spirit. We cannot fix people. It is not our job. Of course, this does not mean that we become passive about sin. It does not mean we condone an unacceptable lifestyle. It simply means that we adhere to biblical principles and procedures for personal transformation.

What God Do You Model?

Our primary role in leading someone into godly transformation is to model the character of God. We should show people love and acceptance. We should extend mercy. We should give them the truth in a way that does not lower their self-worth. We should model unfailing love. We should allow them to see the forbearance of God through us. In this kind of emotional environment, the Holy Spirit can speak to their hearts and draw them to God.

Unfortunately, we are all modeling the god we believe in. Idolatry in the New Testament is seldom a person cutting down a tree, fashioning it into an idol, bowing before it, and saying, "You are my god." Instead, Christian idolatry is when one creates a false image of God in his own heart and mind. When we see God differently than Jesus presented Him, we are idolaters. As a result, we serve the god of our imagination while rejecting God the Father of the Lord Jesus, whom Jesus clearly showed us through His life's teaching and model. Again, the god we show the world is the one we believe in.

A scriptural principle says, "You become what you behold." Psalm 34 presents this concept when it talks about magnifying the Lord. We cannot actually make God bigger, as the word *magnify* indicates. But we can make Him bigger in our own hearts and minds by focusing our attention on Him. The Scriptures teach that it is in His presence that we are transformed.

In 1 John 3, the Bible teaches that seeing Jesus as He is will be the power that transforms us. This transformation happens on a daily basis and will culminate in a complete change when He returns. On the other hand, the Bible warns against running with ungodly people. It warns against wicked fellowship. It tells us to avoid the presence of sin. It tells us to refuse to listen to teaching that will cause us to err from the truth. (See Proverbs 13:20; 1 Thessalonians 5:22; and 2 Timothy 4, for example.)

These admonitions are based on the principle that "what you behold, you become." Whatever we hold in our mental focus for extended periods of time draws us and ultimately conforms us to its image. This principle can work for us or against us. God gave us this ability for good, but too often we use it for our own destruction.

We want to be like God, and that is good. The problem is in our concept of God. You see, you become like the god you believe in. Sadly, the voice of condemnation that you hear in your heart is neither the voice of the devil nor the voice of God; it is the voice of self-criticism. Religion has taught you that it was the voice of God, but it is not.

At this moment, we all are expressing outwardly what we are experiencing inwardly. If we are experiencing condemnation in our hearts, then we can't help but express condemnation to the world around us. If we feel scrutinized, we will in turn scrutinize. But if we feel love and acceptance, we will give love and acceptance.

To Know God Is to Know Love

The Bible says, *"Everyone who loves has been born of God and knows God. Whoever does not love does not know God, because God is love"* (1 John 4:7–8 NIV). The word *know* comes from the Greek word *ginosko.* This word speaks of an experiential knowledge; it is experienced and felt. Since God is love, He gives love. If we are actually experiencing God, we will feel loved. If we are feeling something other than love, we are not experiencing God. Likewise, if we are not giving love, it is simply because we are not experiencing love from God in our own hearts.

Jesus said, *"Freely you have received, freely give"* (Matthew 10:8 NIV). One of the reasons people do not give the love of God freely is that they have never freely received it. They think they are laboring under God's scrutiny. As a result, their natural reaction is to give scrutiny.

Not only are externalists out of touch with their hearts, but they are also afraid to look in their hearts. They need to keep the focus outward because they are afraid of whom they will see inside. They are afraid they will look in their hearts and find the mean, critical god they believe in. The truth is, once they get past their vain imaginations regarding Him, they will find their loving heavenly Father, the God of all mercy and comfort.

Accepting the reality of God's love for me delivers me from the need to find fault with others. My sense of security is now the product of a relationship with God in my heart. As I relate to God from my heart and experience the empowerment of love and acceptance, I will be more apt to model that love to others. I also will point others to God in their hearts instead of pointing to their behavior. Now I can love you instead of blame you!

Eight

The Critical Eye

⚜

How I see you is a reflection of how I see me.

Jesus asked, *"Why do you look at the speck of sawdust in your brother's eye and pay no attention to the plank in your own eye?"* (Matthew 7:3 NIV). Christians seem to be uncontrollably motivated by some deep need to "take the dog by the ears." (See Proverbs 26:17.) They are always meddling in other people's stuff. This is one of the main reasons the world hates the church. We have declared ourselves to be the world's police force. We are the self-proclaimed militant army that is here to police and judge the world, when we should be a loving family who brings hurting people into the family circle by adoption!

Our concept of presenting what we mistakenly call the Gospel is to let people know they are sinners so they will realize their need for Jesus. This erroneous concept leads the Christian to think that the best way to let people know they are sinners is to point out their faults—that is, to find the speck in their eye.

Your Heart Dictates How You See

The way we view something is the product of our heart. If we have a critical eye, it is because we have a critical heart. The Bible says, *"He that hath a froward heart findeth no good"* (Proverbs 17:20). A *"froward heart"* is a crooked heart. It is a heart that has been reshaped through the pressures of sin, legalism, religion, or life circumstances. It is a heart that sees only the bad; it cannot find the good.

Some people seem to have mistaken criticism for discernment. Criticism is not a gift of the Holy Spirit; it is the product of a corrupt heart. Religion has forged the church into a critical, reactionary society not much different than that of the Pharisees in Jesus' day.

Christians have created an antagonistic relationship with the world. Today the church is reaping the scrutiny and judgment that it has sown for seventeen hundred years. It is no wonder the world hates us and looks for fault in us! It is merely repaying our investment—with interest. We are reaping the seeds of judgment and criticism that have been sown for centuries.

Our need to find fault does not, however, stop with the world. We also have turned our scrutiny onto our brothers and sisters in the Lord. We try to motivate other believers to grow by showing them how weak and faulty they are. Not only do we police their actions, but we also police their words. We try to make them observe the right formulas for confession and prayer. As a result, we have made the church a very unsafe place even for believers who are in need. In fact, our list of rules has probably become as long as that of the Pharisees.

Those around us will always have needs in their lives, just as we will always have needs. But just because we see the need in another person does not mean we have the right to invade that individual's life. Our first goal should be to love the person and make him feel safe while owning his problem. If people do not feel safe with their problem, they will feel that they have to cover it up. They also certainly will not respond positively to our inquisition! We actually force people into denial by our rejection and condemnation. When they see our disapproval and rejection of people with problems, they realize that we will reject them because of their problems as well. They see that it is not safe for them to expose their problems to our critical eye.

Someone once said, "The person who will influence you most is not the person you believe in; it is the person who believes in you." There is a question we need to ask ourselves: Can we still see the good in people who have obvious problems? Do we make people see that we believe in them even with their problems?

Some People See God Only through Us

Colossians 4:6 says, *"Let your conversation be always full of grace, seasoned with salt, so that you may know how to answer everyone"* (NIV). God's grace is His ability that works in us. Our speech should always convey ability and empowerment. It should make people completely confident that they can do all things through Christ. When they are under our scrutiny, we should see the power of God in them instead of the weakness of the flesh, and we must let them know that we are confident of Christ in them.

Paul said that our talk should be salty. Salt has many great qualities, but as much as anything else it is a preserver. Our speech should preserve people, not destroy them. Once we have negatively touched a person's self-worth, all meaningful communication is over. Jesus never attacked self-worth. Even in the most outrageous cases, He was merciful. He was kind and patient. No example makes this clearer than when He encountered the woman taken in adultery. (Read John 8 to get the full story.)

The goal in our every conversation, the goal for all our ministry, must be to bring people to a loving experience with God. That experience, however, begins with what they encounter in us. Our interactions with people cannot be about proving them wrong or proving ourselves right. Such thinking is at the heart of removing the splinter from our brother's eye while ignoring the board in our own. No, our job is to persuade them of God's love so they will feel safe enough to trust Him. They do not need to expose their heart to us; they need to expose their heart to God.

People also experience God by watching us model the kind of life they can have. People learn far more from what they see in us than from what they hear from us. They need to see that we handle with happiness and peace the same issues they have. Albert Schweitzer said, "Example is not the main thing in influencing others. It's the only thing." Jesus knew this; His ministry followed a pattern of teaching, discussing, modeling, discussing, assisting, discussing, sending forth, and discussing. He lovingly and patiently led His disciples through the process of personal development. Although their flaws were evident, He stuck to principle-based teaching that led people to the place of self-discovery. It was always safe to be real around Jesus. It was always safe to ask questions, and it was always safe to discuss the issues.

The critical eye sees a fault and, in the name of love and ministry, begins to pluck up the tares, or weeds, in a negative attempt to remove the problem. In the end, the devastation is so great that the field (the heart) is destroyed. Jesus warned of the devastation that comes from trying to solve problems by pulling out the tares; He warned that the wheat would be pulled out as well. (See Matthew 13.) So a fault-finding, critical eye finds what it judges to be the problem and begins to pull it out. But in the process, the wheat is destroyed, and the person is left with nothing.

When I am delivered from a critical eye, I will see people as God sees them. I will always know that the Spirit of God can work in them to solve every problem and conquer every obstacle. You see, our confidence in people is directly related to our confidence in God. When we see the best in them, they will see, believe, and live the best God has to offer.

Nine

Knowing the
Boundaries

✦❧✦

If I don't know me, it is impossible for me to know you.

The concept of boundaries is somewhat foreign to the religious mind-set. Boundaries establish limits over which no one should venture. Some boundaries are established by the Bible to provide basic and essential guidelines for healthy relationships. Failing to observe those boundaries always results in pain and dysfunctional relationships. Sometimes people invite us to step over a boundary, but there are some boundaries we should never cross, even when invited. Judgment is one of these. Trying to fix another person is stepping over a line we should never cross.

Even the simple desire to help a person could cause us to cross boundaries uninvited. Someone once said, "The difference between a pest and a welcome guest is an invitation." If a relationship does not promote the kind of trust that inspires a person to invite us into his or her life, we have no real ministry opportunity.

Let me give you an example. In the early years of my marriage, I used my behavior as a standard to judge my wife's behavior. Naturally, my judgment left me as being the more "spiritual" one. I am also more verbal than my wife is. So when we had problems, I always wanted to talk them out. I cannot tell you how many times I created a family war because I crossed those boundaries uninvited. I didn't listen when she said, "I don't want to talk." Instead, I forced my way into an area that she was not ready to open to me. In the process, I pushed us farther apart.

As the years went by, I learned to respect her boundaries. I have found that when I am a welcome guest across those lines, I have been able to talk about anything. As an annoying, uninvited pest, I simply create pain and conflict for both of us.

Communicate Effectively—Love People

We Christians have an important message. In fact, it is the most important thing a person could ever hear. Unfortunately, it seems we often let the importance of our message justify our violating every scriptural principle of communication. God's Word is full of teaching about how to communicate effectively. But because we do not respect people and are not motivated by love, we disregard those Scriptures. If we trusted God's wisdom, we would present our message in a manner that utilized every positive communication skill possible.

When Saul first began his ministry, as related in the book of Acts, his communication skills were still those of a legalistic Pharisee. He caused so much trouble in Jerusalem that persecution broke out against him and the church. The brothers eventually took him, put him on a boat, and sent him away. Then, the Bible says, the churches in that area finally had peace. (See Acts 9:27–31.) This is a far cry from the man who changed his name to the Gentile "Paul," shaved his beard, and ate with the unclean pagans in order to become an invited guest. Paul's respect for the message and the people eventually provoked him to walk in love and wisdom for the greatest benefit of the people.

We must realize that every time we violate any principle of communication, we reduce the effectiveness of our message. Ignoring those principles sends a message to the person with whom we wish to communicate that says, "You are of no value." Our message may be the Gospel, or it may be a deep relational need. Regardless of the content, if we want it to be received, it must be communicated in a meaningful way. Rarely do people reject real communication. It is our rude, ill-equipped, condemning, or negative approach to communication that people reject. When we value people, we put forth the effort necessary to communicate in a way that will be acceptable and effective.

It Is None of My Business

Proverbs 26:17 says, *"He who passes by and meddles in a quarrel not his own is like one who takes a dog by the ears"* (NKJV). A problem is not ours just because it affects us. Judgment causes us to fail to recognize boundaries. When another's behavior affects us, we consider that fact alone to be enough justification to reject biblical wisdom. We tend to follow a logic that says, "If it affects me, it is my business." That is not true. It is only our judgment that causes us to take ownership of another person's actions. "That was about me." "He did that to hurt me." "If she really loved me, she would never do that." All of these are judgments that cause the actions of others to become ours. This, then, gives us an imaginary license to invade their boundaries.

Our justification is that "so-and-so offended me," but what we think is an offense may not be a real offense. An offense is something that causes you to stumble. People offend you only when they deliberately attempt to make you stumble. Getting your feelings hurt is not an offense. Feeling ignorant around someone is not an offense. Being made angry is not an offense. Most of those experiences come as a by-product of our judgment. They may not have been the intention of the other person.

It Is Your Choice

I must know where I stop and you start. I must always seek to work on my issues and attitudes with God in my heart. I can never make you responsible for my actions or reactions. Likewise, I can never allow you to drag me into your stuff. I must never allow you to make me responsible for your choices. The cry of every abuser is, "Look what you made me do!" No one makes you do anything. You make choices.

Let me expand on this a little bit. The abuser is a touchy, angry person who judges that the people around him do what they do as an act of personal aggression. The perceived aggression has power over the abuser because of his judgments. He feels that his boundaries have been invaded. His dignity has been assaulted. Thus, his reaction is the righteous vindication of his judgment.

If you are in a hostile environment, make a choice. Choose to stay or choose to leave. But let that choice be *your* choice. Make it based on what you want in life. If you leave, do so in peace and with as much love as possible. If you stay, do so in peace and love. Above all, free yourself from the control of others by making your own choices and recognizing your own boundaries.

Whatever you do, however, do not cross boundaries—regardless of the sincerity of your intention. Good intentions do not make foolishness valid. When something affects you, make your choices about how you want to relate to it without succumbing to the need to cross the boundaries uninvited. When people want you to cross, they will invite you. When they invite you to a place into which the Word of God forbids entry, don't go!

Ten

God of My World

❧

If I give you control of my life, I make you my god.

Matthew 7:4 says, *"How can you say to your brother, 'Let me take the speck out of your eye,' when all the time there is a plank in your own eye?"* (NIV). It seems that we cannot resist the temptation to fix others. Yet, in our attempts to fix, we often destroy. Every day marriages are lost and friendships ruined in people's futile attempts to fix the other person. What causes us to hurt those we intend to help? It is largely because we are blinded by the plank in our own eye. You see, we have our own issues. We, too, deal with sin. Of course, it is not just the fact that we have sin in our lives that blinds us in helping others. No, the Bible says, *"If we say that we have no sin, we deceive ourselves"* (1 John 1:8, emphasis added). The context suggests that it is the judgment in our lives that is the real plank. The idea that I have the "right" to judge is a major problem. Regardless of the other person's problem, this one is just as big and potentially more destructive for me.

Judgment, when trying to help another, is like a patient going to a doctor and the doctor deciding why the patient is sick without an examination. The doctor may have good intentions for prescribing surgery, but if it is the wrong surgery, it will not be appreciated. Judgment works the same way. We decide why people do what they do. We determine what their "real" problems are, and then we begin to "operate."

Control Is Not an Option

In the original temptation in the Garden of Eden, Adam was offered the opportunity to be god of his own world. We find this desire at the heart of many of our personal conflicts, subtly embedded in our motives. Of course, none of us thinks we are exercising this as a prerogative. No Christian would dare set himself up as god. Yet it happens daily. The moment I judge or control, I have set myself up as god.

The god of any system is the one who determines what is good and what is evil. So instead of accepting God's determination of good and evil, we look at what the person did, then ask ourselves why he did it. Then, based on why we think he did it, we determine it to be good or evil. That journey into judgment is the act of enthroning ourselves as god of our system. We all have our own "world system"—it is the system we use to attempt to control our environment.

In our "world system," not only do we have the right to judge, but our judgment also gives us the right to control. Naturally, we have good intentions in our desire to control. We really think that if the other person gave us control, we could make his or her life much better. Those intentions are usually based on our judgments, however, and it is essential that we realize control is never a suitable option.

To be blunt, control is a form of witchcraft. Paul told the Galatian believers that they had been bewitched (Galatians 3:1). They had been brought under the control of the Judaizers. Of course, the Judaizers had justification for their control. In their minds, they were acting on behalf of God. The problem is, God never uses control to accomplish His will in the earth. He works through the hearts of people. He leads and instructs us as the children He loves. If control was God's method, He could solve the world's problems in one decisive act.

Control Starts with Judgment

Judgment is always a part of the process of control. It is judgment that causes us to feel that we have the right to control others. Judgment justifies any negative or evil behavior we choose to act out. It is the pathway to personal idolatry. Our judgments, when imposed, cause people to bow to our wills.

If you are god of your world, you are living under a lot of stress. If you are the one who imposes changes through control, then you are the one who has to keep all those changes in place. The most stressed-out person in the family is usually the controller. That individual's constant lament is, "I have to do everything!"

That complaint may be true. After all, a controller immobilizes people. He or she robs others of the freedom to act independently. So all the decisions fall back on the shoulders of the controlling leader—father, mother, or spouse.

When we usurp the Lordship of Jesus in the life of another, it is impossible for that person to experience God's grace, which empowers him to make the needed changes. It is a cycle of disappointment and failure. We want our friends and family to change, but we become the main obstacle in their process of change.

Eventually, when people fail to change, we create new judgments about why they are not changing. Those judgments usually bring more pain and disappointment to our own lives. We think they don't love us. Or maybe they're just lazy! When we reach a verdict, we begin to carry out our sentencing as if our judgment is reality.

While we are involved in our own judgments, the other person has his own judgments and reactions going. As a result, the relationship is polarized even more, and people push each other farther and farther apart. As the pain level increases, we become less willing to take productive steps. Soon the relationship, friendship, or marriage is over. Sadly, few people ever divorce over the real issues. They divorce over their judgments.

We read these words, and our first thought is of how they apply to others. We think that our desire to do things right excuses us from the wisdom of God's Word. We falsely assume that a good motive is reason enough to reject that Word. Remember, it does not matter why you are trying to control; it is still wrong! Submit yourself to the Lordship of Jesus. Apply truth to yourself, and let each person answer to God for himself, independent of your control. Stop being god, and free yourself from the pressure!

Eleven

How I See It

❧

How I see it is not how it is; it is just how I see it.

I recently read an article that someone wrote about me. It was scathing, slanderous, and mostly untrue. Fortunately, the person was kind enough not to use my name. When my staff saw the article, though, they were deeply offended for me. They wanted to print a rebuttal and tell my side of the story. They wanted the truth to come out. I knew it would be of no value to attempt reasoning with the writer, however; what he had written was not true, but it was all that he was able to see.

One of the most important lessons I ever learned was this: "How I see it is not how it is; it is just how I see it." Reality is distorted by our perception. Our perception, in turn, is forged by many subjective factors, the most central being our self-worth. We see and interpret the world around us based on how we see ourselves. People with poor self-worth interpret the information they receive in a negative way—one that tends to make them the victim.

It's like the old joke about the guy who goes to a football game. At the beginning of the game, he jumps up and runs angrily out of the stadium. When his friend catches up with him, the friend asks, "Why did you leave?" The man says, "It was too painful." "What was too painful?" "When they all got in that little group and talked about me."

As silly as that joke is, it is nothing compared to the bizarre reactions that people have when they falsely assume they are being attacked.

My stepfather was a very violent, insecure man. He always thought people were trying to prove he was stupid. Most of the time, when there was conflict, it began with him shouting, "Do you think I'm stupid or something?" What he never realized was that *he* was the one who thought he was stupid. I witnessed a lifetime of extreme violence that was the result of his judgments. More than once I saw him violently attack complete strangers for simply looking at him. His judgment said, "They are looking at me because they think I'm stupid."

The more negative people's sense of self-worth is, the more judgmental their attitude. Remember, judgment always asks why. People who feel victimized always want to know why. Because they experience low self-worth, they always answer that question in a negative, subjective manner.

If you do not think well of yourself, you will also think that others do not think well of you. You then judge all their actions in light of this negative self-perception. If you think you are not likable, then you judge others' actions based on that preconceived idea. If you are fearful or paranoid, you think others do things to "get" you. These negative judgments, based on your self-perception, become the reality you experience, regardless of the intentions of other people.

I See Life through My Opinions

Self-centeredness is present in every sin. Now, self-centeredness is not always the obvious "make me first" attitude.

Self-centeredness simply makes self the focal point for interpreting life and its events. On one end of the spectrum, a self-centered person may be the bully who takes from others and never considers the pain he inflicts. On the other end is the person with a negative self-perception who interprets everything in light of herself. This person sees herself as the center of the world she has created, and people in her world do what they do because of her. One seems arrogant, and the other humble, but they are both self-absorbed.

When people pass a judgment or develop strong opinions, they lock themselves into selective processing. Studies show that forming strong opinions causes activity in the reticular activating system, which is located at the base of the skull. This neurological activity produces a mental state in which one can see only what he or she has predetermined. In other words, you no longer see it how it is. Your mind selectively processes information that confirms your perception while ignoring data that is contrary to your point of view. We all have done this. We all have looked at a label and were sure that it said one thing, only to later discover that it said something completely different.

The mind seeks equilibrium. It seeks to validate your opinions. Once you make a judgment about a person, whether good or bad, you will notice only what validates your judgment. You will interpret all the person's actions on the basis of that judgment. For example, let's say that you see a woman dressed in extremely bright-colored clothes. She has bleached hair, and maybe her dress is just a little too tight. You decide she is an immoral person. That is your reasoning/judgment about why she is dressed in such a manner.

As you observe her, you see her approach several men. You notice how she stands a little too close to them when she talks. She brazenly looks them directly in the eye. Your opinion is now confirmed. She is an immoral person—probably a prostitute—and you have seen her approaching men. But what you didn't notice was the handful of tracts she was carrying. She was, in fact, sharing her faith with people. These kinds of blind judgments happen every day and distort our experience. We overlook the obvious once we have made up our minds.

Once you pass a judgment on someone, you then experience the person and the event based on your judgment. Regardless of the other person's intentions, your experience with him or her is based on your judgment. Remember the example in an earlier chapter of the pastor walking past you without speaking to you one Sunday morning? All he did was walk past you, but your judgment determined whether you were offended or whether it was an insignificant event. You see, the aggression we feel from others may have nothing to do with them—but it has everything to do with us. So the pastor walking by you cannot cause you pain. The judgment you pass, though, can cause incredible pain.

Your Feelings Overshadow Actual Events

In the 1970s, I was speaking to a group about starting a Christian school. I was talking about the need for parental involvement, and I used the example of a single mother who, because of her work schedule, was never able to be at home in the evening to work with her son. Consequently, he seldom did his homework and got in a lot of trouble. Eventually he had to be released from school. The lack of parental support made him impossible to help.

In the audience was a grandmother who was a major contributor to the new school and had a son who had just gone through a bitter divorce. She had a granddaughter whom she loved passionately. She was defensive and embarrassed about the divorce, and this defensiveness caused her to pass a lot of judgments. In her mind, she thought I had said that children of divorced parents could not go to our school. She was furious. I could not convince

63

her that I had not, in any way, indicated this. She, however, knew what she had heard. The pastor came over, politely listened to her, then assured her that she had misunderstood. "No," she replied, "I know what I heard." We even gave her the tape and let her listen to it. She was convinced that it had been erased from the tape. After all, she knew what she had heard.

The sad thing is, she did hear what she thought she heard. But I didn't say it. She heard it in her own mind. Her fears made her oversensitive to anything referring to divorce. The moment I began talking about single parents, she probably passed a judgment. That judgment affected her ability to process information. Her experience was real to her, but it just wasn't true. She never liked me after that event, and she told others what she had "heard" me say.

As far as she was concerned, she was not lying every time she repeated that story. That was the way she had experienced the event. You see, you never remember what actually happened; you remember how it made you feel. How many times have your kids said, "You were yelling at me"? You weren't yelling at them, but that is what they experienced.

The misunderstanding doesn't stop there, however. Every time you remember something, your experience of the event may change. Not only do you remember how it made you feel, instead of how it actually happened, but your memory also changes every time you think of it again. The next time you tell the story, you remember it the way it made you feel the last time you remembered it. This is how most exaggerations grow.

Repentance Brings a New View

Our minds will allow us to see something from a different viewpoint only when we release our judgments. It is like the three boys who peeped through the holes in a circus tent to look at the elephant and disagreed on what they saw. One said an elephant looked like a long, skinny snake. The other argued that it had big wings. The third insisted that it looked like a big tree trunk. They all had seen the elephant, but each had seen it from a different position. One saw the tail, the other the ears, and the other the legs. Because they all were so sure of what they had seen, they refused to look through another hole in the tent.

All it takes to see something differently is to look at it from a different position. For us, the hole in the tent may be our fear, prejudice, or anger. It is the framework through which we view something. Again, our experience is real; it is just based on limited or distorted information. We must be willing to surrender our opinion before we can see it another way. This is what the Bible calls repentance—to have a change of mind. In repentance, we must be willing to release the way we see something. Then we are free to look at it from another position.

Most of the time we tend to hold on to our point of view. By now we have taken a stand; we have invested in it emotionally. Repentance may mean we have to admit to being wrong. The mind would rather preserve its opinion. The ego wants to be right. We say that we want to see the truth, but we are not willing to suffer the risk of being wrong. Now we have an irreconcilable difference. At this point, a revelation from God will have no effect on us.

A revelation from God is not His showing us something new; a revelation is simply what we see when we are flexible enough to change our mental/emotional position about an issue and look at it from a different point of view. God doesn't show us something He previously kept hidden; we see something He wanted to show us all along.

Only the pure in heart will see God, according to Matthew 5:8. So keep your heart pure from judgment, prejudice, and bias. Let go of your predetermined ideas, and you may see a lot of hurtful events differently. When you feel defensive or angry, remind yourself, "This is only how I see it. I must see it from another position to overcome this offense." Then, discover another point of view.

Twelve

Identifying Behavior Patterns

-᎐ᏋᏋ᎐

People don't do things for my reasons; they have their own.

One of the greatest assumptions that leads us into judgment is the idea that people do things for the same reasons we do them. In behavioral studies we see that there are four basic behavioral styles, which are then divided into more than a hundred complex patterns. These four are the *direct,* the *inspirational,* the *steady,* and the *conscientious* persons.* Each of these behavioral styles communicates in a different manner. They interpret their world in different ways. They are motivated by entirely different factors. But most importantly, they make judgments based on different perceptions.

For example, the direct person prefers to get to the point. He wants to know the bottom line, and he has a strong force of character. The direct man or woman deeply desires to be respected. The inspirational pattern is a "people person." This person is easily inspired and easily discouraged. Her goal in life is to be

* DISC Carlson Learning Co. *The DISC Profile.* Minneapolis, Minn.: Inscape Publishing, 1986, 1995.

liked; she is looking for social acceptance. The steady person is very kind and personable. A steady person tends to remain calm and is good at calming excited people. She is very indirect, avoids conflict, and seeks to keep things steady. The conscientious person is analytical and detail-oriented. This type considers himself to be the quality control person. He wants everything to be right. Diplomatic and disliking direct conflict, he seeks to control through the use of quality standards.*

You Don't Think like I Think, but I Think You Do

Any of these people may do the same things. However, they are usually motivated by completely different reasoning. A direct person would be most apt to lie in order to maintain respect. An inspirational person would lie to maintain social acceptance. The steady person would lie to avoid conflict, and the conscientious person to appear to be right. All of us struggle with the same temptations, but it is essential to realize that each of us is motivated by completely different needs, fears, and desires. We can never really know what drives another person's behavior. But we think we do—and this causes a great deal of pain and conflict.

The problem in conflict resolution is that people usually fail to understand why others do what they do. The effect of their actions on us comes from the erroneous judgment that "people do things for the same reason I do things." When we make this assumption, we project our values and reasons onto others. We begin to treat them as if our judgment is correct. This usually leads to more conflict. I have seen hundreds of marriages saved when a husband and wife simply accept that they each do things for their own reasons. Their actions are not personal; they would do the same things regardless of whom they married.

---

* For more information on the four basic patterns, contact Impact International School of Ministry at the address on the copyright page.

For example, direct people prefer a lot of personal space. Their personal space is quite large. They make direct eye contact, but they keep their distance. Physical contact is kept to a minimum. Many interpret this distance to be rejection. The inspirational pattern, on the other hand, is very touchy-feely. If they are distant to someone, it means that they dislike or are uncomfortable with that person.

Keeping that in mind, suppose a direct woman sees an inspirational woman standing close to others, touching them while talking, and being very personable. She projects her motives onto the inspirational person and reasons, "If I were making that much physical contact, I would have sexual intent." Her judgment concerning why the inspirational woman relates so physically takes the quantum leap: "She does that because she is immoral." Many inspirational people have a reputation for being flirty or immoral simply because others project their own motives onto the situation.

Now suppose the inspirational woman begins to talk to the direct man. She notices how far away he stands. She also notices that if she steps toward him, he backs away. This, of course, makes her feel rejected, so she steps even closer. After all, she would only back away from someone who makes her feel uncomfortable. As a result, when he backs up once again, she assumes that Mr. Direct does not like her. He, on the other hand, perceives her natural inclination to make him feel more comfortable as being flirty. Both people are using their personal behavior as a standard of judgment for the other. Both will begin to respond to the other as if their judgment is correct. They may even create the problem they fear.

In another case, let's say a direct man calls a steady man. The direct man wants to be polite. He recognizes that he is invading the steady person's space. Out of his intention to be kind, he gets to the point. After all, he is a "bottom-liner." If any personal conversation happened, it would come after the point was made. So he calls and says something like this: "Bob? Jim here. How are you? Bob, I need to borrow your projector for a presentation on Saturday. Is that a problem?" He has communicated in this concise manner because he thinks that what he prefers is what everyone else prefers.

Remember, steady people are very indirect. They are also very personable. They would never call you and go straight for the bottom line unless they disliked you or were angry. In their attempt to be kind, they would be personal first. They would seek to make you feel special by showing interest in you and your family. They would ask all sorts of personal questions before getting to the point. They, too, assume that everyone does everything for the same reasons.

Because Jim (Mr. Direct) did not inquire about Bob's (Mr. Steady's) family or ask him anything personal, Bob assumes that Jim is angry. Remember, Jim got to the point in an attempt to be courteous. Bob is offended. When he tells this story to others, he will tell what he experienced. "Jim called me the other day and was so rude and inconsiderate." That is not what happened, but it is what Bob experienced because of his judgment: "If I did it that way, this is what it would mean."

Now look at it the other way around. "Jim, this is Bob. How are you? Are Brenda and the girls doing well? I haven't seen them lately." All the while Jim is thinking, *Why don't you tell me what you really want?* Bob is attempting to be thoughtful and kind. But because Jim would only be this indirect if he was attempting to manipulate someone, he feels manipulated. He becomes very agitated with Bob. The greatest fear of the direct person is of being manipulated. He or she feels that if you don't get straight to the point, you are manipulating. Jim's judgment of why Bob is communicating this way would lead him to believe, feel, and react as if he was being manipulated.

70

Understand the Difference

Direct and inspirational people tend to talk in generalities. Conscientious, or analytical, people never talk in generalities; they tend to go overboard on the details. They tend to treat every conversation as if it were a report—an admirable trait when used in a conference room. But it is not admirable in a casual conversation or when telling a story. The analytical person thinks that direct or inspirational people are lying when they speak in generalities. After all, the detail-oriented person would speak in generalities only when attempting to avoid the details. On the other hand, when the direct person is overrun with so many details, he or she may feel that the analytical person is being pushy or manipulative. The examples could be endless. The problem, however, is simple. People do not do things for our reasons. Yet, because of our judgment, we treat them as if they do. Our conflict is seldom based on what a person does. It is usually based on our judgment of why he did it.

Too often we judge people and create conflict, only to eventually discover that our judgment was wrong. Then we're too late! The damage is already done. So often we cheat ourselves out of many wonderful friendships because of initial judgments. We meet and reject people before we ever get to know them. And what we do know about them is seldom who they are; it is our judgment of who they are.

Perhaps the worst place this happens is in our relationships with our children. Direct people are multitasked. If their children are not, they judge the children to be lazy or stupid. Steady people are overwhelmed by long lists but do very well when given a few tasks at a time. Analytical parents make judgments about their inspirational children and so often fail to meet their children's need for physical affection. They also constantly criticize their children's lack of follow-through, while totally overlooking their creativity and warmth.

The Bible says, *"All the ways of a man are clean in his own eyes"* (Proverbs 16:2). We think we are right. We think our way is *the* way. That is why we do things the way we do them. We also want our children to be right, and so we think our children should be like us. If they are not, we judge their actions as being motivated by rebellion, ignorance, or deceit. They are none of those things. What makes us intolerant of adults who behave differently than we do is the same thing that makes us intolerant of our children when they are not our behavioral clones—judgment!

When we release people from our judgment, we will be able to know them for who they are. We will come to value how they are different from us. We will end the cycle of sowing and reaping pain!

Thirteen

Destroying Every New Relationship

-◦Ɛ◦-

I want it the way it has always been, but different.

U sing our life experiences as our basis, we establish a paradigm of the world. As we go through various experiences, we make judgments. In other words, we determine why these things happen. And because we have a sin nature, we always make that determination from a self-centered perspective: Why did that happen to me?

When we were children, we tended to judge every experience in light of what it meant about us. Through a sin/fear nature, we interpreted every event in our lives as if it were all about us. Then we interpreted the world through our judgment of those experiences. Some studies indicate that our self-perception is established before we reach the age of five. Think about that. We developed our view of the world through our experiences and subjective judgments long before we ever reached adulthood.

The Scriptures teach that all children are born with a sin nature. This does not mean that every child desires to be evil or commit sin; it simply means that every child is born inherently fearful. (One leading child psychologist believes that fear is the only inborn emotion a child possesses.) The sin nature revolves around self. Because the nature of fear is subjective, fear puts "me" at the center of a person's experience. Therefore, the person with a sin nature interprets everything subjectively, making it "all about me."

We Must Renew Our Minds

Our subjective worldview is established before we are mature enough to realize that *not* everything is about us. Even when we do realize that not everything is about us, we fail to realize that our worldview was established in such a self-centered manner. We don't know where we got our view of the world; we just know that this is the way we see things, and it forms the basis of our self-perception and all our actions.

This is why it is so essential that believers renew their minds. We must interpret the world in light of our new identity in Jesus. We must look at the world after we have placed Him at the center. We can no longer be the matrix from which we determine our understanding of the world. We must release the world from our sinful, self-centered judgment. That means we must reconsider all past interpretations and release our past judgments of all people and events. Otherwise we will be locked into our current views and opinions, making it impossible for us to renew our minds.

Our concepts of father, mother, mate, and maybe even friend are already established. By our experiences and judgments we have, to a certain degree, cast our lot in life even before we reach puberty. Apart from a change of heart, most of our major decisions in life are predetermined by how we view the world and ourselves.

Children who grow up in homes where criticism is the norm will live the rest of their lives out of the judgments they make about criticism. A boy may judge, "My mother criticized me because she loved me." That judgment may predetermine what kind of woman he will marry. When he longs for love, he will look for someone who criticizes him. After all, that is his judgment concerning his mother's criticism. Criticism equals love, in his view. But then he cannot understand why he is miserable in this adult relationship.

The girl who passes a judgment that all criticism is a form of rejection will be forced in another direction. She will avoid anyone who attempts to add any quality or direction to her life. She may search out a mate who has no opinion, is afraid of confrontation, and never shares his view. She could be doomed to a life with a non-communicator. Unhappy with this person who seems so "emotionless," she doesn't understand why she was ever attracted to him.

What Relationships Are Really All About

Because we have already decided how the roles in life should be played out, we approach new relationships looking for our idea of a friend. We already have a definition of what type of person this will be. Much of this is done on a subconscious level. It is, however, clearly directing the course of our lives—and it all revolves around judgments. This explains why, when teaching about the heart, Jesus said that what we have, we'll get more of—whether good or bad (Mark 4:24–25). Unless we sow the Word in our hearts and change the beliefs of our hearts, we are doomed to repeat the patterns of our past and relive the same painful experiences.

Relationships should be places of personal development. They should challenge and stimulate us. They should open us to the many new facets of life. When we get to know new and different people, we have the opportunity to grow as never before. Our problem, however, is that we pass so many judgments before we really get to know new people that we seldom allow those outside of our paradigm into our emotional circle.

We have views of what is a good friend and what is a bad friend. Those views were established by the judgments we made throughout our lives. Based on our views, we will accept or reject a new acquaintance before ever really getting to know the person. This is why people fall into repetitive patterns in their relationships. They have already decided what kind of person they will accept and what kind of person they will reject. This is part of what locks us into following the same destructive patterns in relationships.

Most studies agree that people will never sustain lasting change unless they are "resocialized." The Bible is very clear about the effects that fellowship and socialization have on our thoughts and actions. People who make godly decisions never see them through to the end unless they are socially involved with people who can emotionally support those decisions. Unfortunately, our judgments keep us in the same social circles all our lives, making change virtually impossible.

In this system of socialization, we stay within a predetermined comfort zone. In other words, we keep it the way it has always been and then wonder why nothing changes. Because we are not interacting with different types of people, we are never challenged. We are not forced to grow. When we meet and are attracted to new people, they are the same kinds of people as the old friends from the past. Only the names and appearances have changed.

For the person who is stuck in unhealthy relationships, this cycle falsely confirms their fears and suspicions. They actually come to believe that all people are the same. In other words, they think, *There is no reality beyond my past experience. After all, every person I get involved with is just like the people I have already known.* Thus, judgments about all men, all women, all whites, all blacks, and so on, are falsely reinforced.

We need new relationships with different kinds of people in order to grow and break out of past patterns. We need people with different behavioral styles. We need people with different levels of character. We need to grow to accept all different types of people. Not every direct person will hurt you. Not everything about inspirational people is bad. Get to know new people, and avoid a repeat performance of past pains.

Fourteen

Becoming like Little Children

-᠍ᘏᘎᙚ-

If I am acting like a child, it's because I think like one!

In Proverbs 4:23, the *New Living Translation* says, *"Above all else, guard your heart, for it affects everything you do."* The heart is the guidance system of your life. All that you do emerges from the beliefs of your heart. The heart is also the seat of your being. It is the collective consciousness of all that you are. It is from the beliefs of the heart that your self-perception and worldview emanate.

The *New King James Version* quotes the latter half of that verse in this way: *"for out of it spring the issues of life."* Because the interpretation of who we are abides in our hearts, all that we do, see, and feel is affected by that perception. Our self-perception is the lens that colors our world. It is the filter through which all data is passed and interpreted. It determines how we experience reality. We may momentarily rise above our heart-perception, or we may momentarily sink beneath it, but ultimately we will return to the beliefs of our hearts.

Proverbs 3:1 tells us to store God's commandments in our hearts. Then verse 3 tells us to write certain attitudes and beliefs on our hearts. This verse reveals what the Bible consistently teaches: It is our responsibility to minister to our hearts. The Bible tells us to believe in the heart, hide the Word in our hearts, guard our hearts, guide our hearts, establish our hearts; and here it tells us to write on our hearts. The ministry of the heart is the sole responsibility of the individual, yet few people ever learn how to consistently influence their hearts in a deliberate way. Most of what happens to our hearts is accidental and without choice.

How Do We "Write" on Our Hearts?

So much of what we believe in our hearts about ourselves is the result of negative and positive experiences that were out of our control. We did not choose them, and when they occurred, we did not realize the effect they would have. Much of what we believe about ourselves also is the product of the actions of dysfunctional people. Adults and other children expressed themselves within the sphere of our emotional experience, and we judged those childhood experiences with the perception and understanding of a child. As we grew, we defined our world and our self-perception from those judgments. We thought those people did what they did because of us, when the truth is that they did what they did because of themselves. We just happened to be there.

One main way we write on our hearts is through a combination of emotion and information. For example, people around us act in a way that has nothing to do with us, but we subjectively judge that conduct. We think it is about us. In that emotional state, our judgment, which manifests as our self-talk, becomes the information we experience. "He does that because I am stupid." "She does that because I'm ugly." "People like me only because I am pretty." Our self-talk during these emotional times is the information that becomes written on our hearts.

79

Many times the judgmental words of the dysfunctional offender become the information we process. As these men or women rage out of control and tell us we are ugly, ignorant, or worthless, we accept their judgment as real. The combination of information and emotion writes something on our hearts that we may never escape. Dysfunctional people justify their actions by placing blame. Dysfunctional people attempt to convince their victims that they are the reason for the offensive actions. Unfortunately, we accept that blame as reality. We write it on our hearts. It forges our self-perception and our ultimate view of the world.

What Do We Make Our Children Feel?

As was previously pointed out, children are born with a sin/fear nature. Since fear puts self at the center of the conscious world, every event is subjectively interpreted. Thus, children write beliefs on their hearts about their world and their world's experiences based on that subjectiveness. The self-centeredness/self-awareness of children makes everything in their world seem to be about them.

The hearts of children are extremely vulnerable. Our childhood is supposed to be the time when we develop a healthy view of ourselves and our world. However, healthy perspectives do not happen because a child is given the right information; they are the result of how a child is made to feel.

Our negative, legalistic view of parenting has caused us to make "teaching the child what is right" the ultimate parenting objective. However, truth in a heart filled with low self-worth will never accomplish its goal. Instead, it will be perverted and twisted into some destructive concept. Even if a child learns what is right, the learning experience may have a terribly negative effect on the child. Teaching a child to "be good" usually results in a self-belief that says, "I am bad."

Before Jesus came, the Jews knew that God was almighty. But because they had a sin/fear nature, they were unsure of how He would use that power. Jesus brought us the revelation of God as a loving Father. From the peace and security that comes from knowing God as a loving Father, we trust Him to use His power in a loving, healthy way. Therefore, we see that a sense of security and acceptance must be the environment for learning; otherwise the information may not accomplish its intended goal.

The top objective in parenting should be to make our children feel loved, accepted, and secure. In that environment, they will be trusting, teachable, and compliant. The goals for raising healthy children and pastoring healthy congregations should be the same. If the heart is safe, it is open and teachable. If there is acceptance, then the reason for teaching is not subjectively twisted into rejection. People should never be taught because they are wrong, but because they are loved.

Parents should model God's love and acceptance to their children. They should make it easy for a child to transition into trusting God without fear. You see, parents are the main source for developing a child's concept of God. Ultimately we come to God and judge Him to be like our parents. If we developed negative concepts of our parents while we were growing up, we come to God as adults with a negative God-concept and a negative self-perception. We think that His Word is given to make us "right." We forget that Jesus made us right by His death and resurrection. We forget that His Word is given to teach us how to live the abundant life. In short, misunderstanding the motive of instruction corrupts the consequences. Parents and pastors should make it their objective to help people experience the love of God before presenting any other aspect of truth.

Having the Heart of a Child

There is a reason why children's hearts are so easily influenced. God created us so that our childhood would be a time of constant learning and development. In professional terms, the meditative state wherein one's heart is easily influenced is called the "alpha state." The alpha state is reached in times of deep prayer, meditation, or simply deep thought and study. In this state, the brain waves slow down to around seven cycles per second. (During the awakened state, brain waves remain at 14 cycles per second or above. This is a state of mind that is more intellectually based and gives the control to the mind, not the heart.) In the alpha state, the conscious mind loses its grip on the thought process, and the thoughts of the heart begin to emerge. The heart also is more vulnerable at this point.

We all enter the alpha state just before entering the sleep state and for a time after awakening in the morning. (I believe this is why such strong emphasis is given to using these times of day to pray.) Although most adults have lost their ability to easily enter the alpha state, children stay in it almost all the time. Some studies indicate that children remain almost constantly in the alpha state until around ten years of age. This means that every experience a child has can potentially affect his or her heart. Maybe this is what Jesus meant when He said, *"I tell you the truth, unless you change and become like little children, you will never enter the kingdom of heaven"* (Matthew 18:3 NIV).

Jesus taught in the parable of the sower that we will keep getting more of what we have, unless we sow something different in our hearts. However, only little children have hearts that are pliable enough to admit the need to grow, change, and develop. Adults insist that they can see, and so they remain in their blindness.

Writing the truth on your heart about who you are in Jesus will not happen accidentally. It will occur as you develop a meditative prayer life that makes establishing your heart the priority. For years I have used a tool that I developed called *The Prayer Organizer* to help people write God's truths on their hearts.

I have seen people go straight from a twenty-year drug addiction to abundant living simply because they took the time to write the truth of their new identity on their hearts. Yet I have also seen those who had relatively "normal" backgrounds never become stable in God. They just didn't have time to develop their hearts. Take the time. It is an investment that will pay dividends for the rest of your life. And the greatest benefit is that it will deliver you from the need to judge.

Fifteen

Life in My Imaginary World

❦

I am god of my own world, and it is killing me!

In the original temptation, Adam was given the opportunity to be god of his own world. He took it. Now, every single day, we live in the fruit of that decision. Every pain, every degree of suffering, every heartache is the result of man choosing to be god of his own world. However, it is not because Adam made that decision thousands of years ago; it is because we exercise that thought as an option in every arena of life's decisions.

We are the center of our universe. We think, *Everything that happens is about me. Everything that befalls me is the result of someone doing something to me.* This is the manifestation of the self-centered world we have created. Then, as we exercise the right to judge, we sustain an illusionary world with "me" at the center. Although it is an illusion, it is one that controls our lives and determines our experiences. Unfortunately, the illusion becomes the reality we experience.

Freed from This World System

Coming to Jesus and being saved from sin encompass far more than the typical religious concept of being saved from doing bad things. Being saved from sin also means that we are redeemed from this sin nature that thrives on fear and self-centeredness. It means we can be saved from this world of pain and chaos we have created. We can be delivered from existing in this painful world and live instead in the kingdom of God.

When the Bible talks about getting free from the world, it is not talking about this "clump of dirt" that floats around in space. It is talking about freedom from the world's system. The world's system is one that operates on principles of self-centeredness, fear, control, and power. It is the system we created by using ungodly principles. More specifically, each of us has created our own world system based on negative principles, and we have placed ourselves at the center as god.

The kingdom of God is a system as well. This system is built on God's principles of love, peace, and joy. It is a system that revolves around Him. In this system we accept Jesus as Lord, He restores us to a relationship with the Father, and we then have the opportunity to live in God's reality, which is the kingdom of God. His kingdom places Him at the center.

We do not automatically enter the kingdom of God when we accept Jesus. Rather, we enter it with every decision we make. Any decision can cause us to experience either God's kingdom system or this world's system. Which system we experience is determined by the principles upon which our decisions are made. If we make decisions by trusting Jesus and His principles, those decisions bring us into the realm of the kingdom of God. When we make decisions by trusting self-centered, fear-based principles, then those decisions thrust us right back into the world's system. They place us once again at the center.

The Heart of the System

How do we get out of the world's system? A commitment to Jesus' Lordship is the only way to be delivered from the old system of death and suffering. When we accept Jesus as Lord, we give up our right to be god of our world. When we give up the throne, we also must surrender our right to judge. In other words, we surrender our views and opinions to His. We accept His wisdom above ours. So accepting Jesus as Lord and yielding to His Lordship in our decision-making process give us access into the kingdom of God and all His reality.

Matthew 7:2 says, *"And with what measure ye mete, it shall be measured to you again."* How we measure out judgment becomes the experiential measure that comes back to us. And it comes back not just as a measure of judgment, but of life. For instance, if I apply judgment to a person's actions, then I have measured it back to myself in a way that alters my experience. If I judge as if everything is about me, then I experience everyone's actions as if they were, in fact, about me. Every unkind thing a person does feels like it is "about me," and it only compounds the pain.

Proverbs 17:20 says, *"He that hath a froward heart findeth no good."* The word *froward*, as I mentioned before, literally means "crooked." The word *crooked* is the same word that is translated as "unrighteous." A righteous heart is straight; an unrighteous heart is crooked. A crooked heart distorts perception. Just as light bends through a prism, reality bends through a crooked heart and is changed in shade and hue. *The Living Bible* says it this way: *"An evil man is suspicious of everyone and tumbles into constant trouble."*

When our hearts are not straight with God's truth and reality, we live in the world of our vain imaginations. We live in a world where the principles of the kingdom of God do not operate. Instead, the principles of fear and self-centeredness rule in this world. It is true that, in Christ, we are saved from this world. However, even though we are saved from it, when we apply the world's principles, it becomes the reality we experience. We can pray as much as we like, but the suffering will not go away. We will not be healed of our pain. You see, God does not come to our vain imaginations to rescue us; He invites us to come to *His* reality, the kingdom of God.

Love is the governing factor in the kingdom of God; fear is the governing factor in the world's system. People who function in self-centeredness are afraid to love. They are afraid that they will be vulnerable, that they will be taken advantage of. They seek to protect themselves by withholding love. They use control and manipulation to obtain the desired result, but it never comes.

Renew Your Mind and Change Your Heart

Paul told the Roman believers that they needed to renew their minds. Renewing their minds would be the only way they could experience the transformation God had promised in Christ. This would be the process through which God would deliver them from pain and bring them to a new reality in Jesus. Like the Roman Christians, we, too, have been given a new spirit. We have been given a new heart. Yet if we continue to think and act on the vain imaginations of our past judgments, we will never experience transformation. We, too, need to renew our minds.

An even more devastating thought is that if we do not renew our minds, we will forge our hearts right back into the same crooked mold that they were in before salvation. Being born again and refusing to renew the mind may get you a ticket to heaven, but the ride will be painful.

The *New Living Translation* says it like this: *"Don't copy the behavior and customs of this world, but let God transform you into a new person by changing the way you think"* (Romans

12:2). Unless we change the way we think, we are forever doomed to wander in the darkness of our old life. That life and its perception were the results of the judgments of a five-year-old child with a sin/fear nature that was totally consumed with self.

Renewing our minds isn't so much about the refusal to think bad thoughts. Rather, renewing our minds is about accepting Jesus as Lord, seeing ourselves the way He says we are, and thereby accepting and experiencing our new identity in Him. Only when we see ourselves as God has created us can we actually see God as He is. Thus the need to renew our minds demands that we release everyone and everything from our past judgments, including ourselves.

The Gospel reveals faith-righteousness from beginning to end. We must start renewing our minds to it by accepting the fact that we are righteous in Jesus. We are completely accepted by God. There is nothing we can do to make ourselves more loved or accepted. Because we are righteous in Jesus, we are loved and accepted. Through these feelings of love, safety, and peace, God can walk us through a life of transformation without us feeling afraid and condemned. (See Romans 5:1.)

As you surrender your right to judge, you release others and yourself from the power and pain of judgment. As you free yourself from judgment, you realize that people do what they do because of what they are experiencing in their own hearts. Their actions have little to do with you. When you surrender and God becomes the center of your world, you see that people do what they do because of where they are with God. If they are experiencing God's love in their hearts, they show love. If they are experiencing something else, they show what is in their hearts. They will manifest their hearts regardless of who is present. Since their actions are not about you, you can love them. You can be patient and kind. For then you realize that their actions do not define who you are. They define who they are.

A "crooked" heart that is not straight with God's reality will lead you to crooked thoughts and crooked results. In light of the promises of God, we cannot accept this substandard life as reality. It is a vain imagination. The only way to free yourself from your imaginary world is to get your heart straight with God by accepting who you are in Jesus. This is the reality you must choose in order to experience the kingdom of God.

Sixteen

Freedom from the Judgment of Others

I'm not who you think I am; I'm not who I think I am. I am who I think you think I am.

—*Unknown*

T he apostle Paul faced painful judgment from the very people whom he had reached with the Gospel. Evidently he was not as eloquent in his speaking skills as Apollos. As is typical for "religious-minded" people, Paul's spirituality was judged on the basis of his ability as an orator. His hearers entered into judgment when they attempted to answer the question, "Why does Apollos preach so much better than Paul?" As a result, Apollos was judged to be more anointed; Paul was judged to be less.

The sad reality was that Apollos wasn't even born again when he preached to these Corinthian believers. He preached John's baptism, not the Gospel (Acts 18:25). Paul, on the other hand, had preached Jesus, and many had been won to the Lord. Yet the Corinthians rejected the reality for the illusion created through their judgments. For many preachers today, this would have been an emotionally crushing event with the potential to alter their destiny.

In 1 Corinthians 4:3, Paul responded to their judgment. *"But with me it is a very small thing that I should be judged of you, or of man's judgment: yea, I judge not mine own self."* It seems that Paul was free from the need to prove himself to others. Their judgments had no power to control his life. His main concern remained the Gospel. His course was not modified to satisfy the opinions of men. But he was able to stay on course with his destiny only because he was free from the power of judgment. Ultimately, at the end of his life, he confidently stated, *"I have fought a good fight, I have finished my course"* (2 Timothy 4:7).

Live Free

In order to fulfill our potential, live our destiny, and realize our dreams, we must live free of the judgments of others. Of course, we should receive input. The Bible teaches that there is value in receiving counsel. *"Plans fail for lack of counsel, but with many advisers they succeed"* (Proverbs 15:22 NIV). We should listen to qualified advisors. But in the end of the decision-making process, we must follow what we believe to be the wisdom of God for us. We will never learn to live out of our hearts or follow the direction of God if we are controlled by the opinions of others.

People who are controlled by judgment feel that others' opinions have power over them. They lash out at people who offer advice. They even accuse others of attempting to control them! In actuality, that feeling of control is the fruit of sowing and reaping. As Matthew 7:2 says, *"And with what measure ye mete, it shall be measured to you again."* People who attempt to control others by judgment feel so controlled themselves that they seldom seek or listen to advice. Such individuals are unrealistically affected by the opinions of others.

"Fearing people is a dangerous trap, but to trust the LORD *means safety"* (Proverbs 29:25 NLT). Foolish people live this Scripture in reverse. They are afraid of God, but they trust people. Judgment controls us when we are more concerned with what people will say than with how God views a situation. Consider the fear of failure. Many different emotional motivations are involved in it, but for many, that fear is based in what others will say "if I fail." That need for approval paralyzes us in our decision making. We don't feel the freedom and empowerment of God; thus, we feel paralyzed in every decision.

Confucius, a Chinese ethical teacher and philosopher who lived from 551–479 B.C., said, "Our greatest glory is not in never falling, but in rising every time we fall." The writer of Proverbs said it this way: *"For though a righteous man falls seven times, he rises again, but the wicked are brought down by calamity"* (Proverbs 24:16 NIV). When asked how he felt about his ten thousand failed attempts to create the light bulb, Thomas Edison responded, "I have not failed. I have just found ten thousand ways that don't work. I am not discouraged, because every wrong attempt discarded is another step forward." Every great inventor and every great leader has had to deal publicly with failure. Those who go on to discover great inventions or to have influential lifestyles are those who are free from the judgments of others.

My father was a perfectionist and an alcoholic. When I was a child, I continually heard him say, "If it is worth doing, then it is worth doing right." Looking back on the legalistic rejection of his parents (my grandparents), I would assume that that type of thinking was part of what drove him to drink. Perfectionism is a torment based on fear. Fear is the fruit of not experiencing love. The perfectionist fears judgment.

This type of thinking dominated the first half of my life. Eventually the need to do right and be right grew into the need to "appear to be right." In time it became more important that others thought I was right than for me to actually be right. I was more concerned with how it looked than how it was. This led to defensiveness, blame shifting, lying, and deceit of all kinds.

At some point in my life I discovered the truth, "If it is worth doing, then it is worth doing wrong until I can learn to do it right." Today I have little concern for what people think compared with my desire to learn and grow as a person, a writer, a disciple, a father, and a husband. We can't grow while covering our tracks. We can't deal with how it is if we are consumed with how it looks.

What Is More Valuable?

Our personal development is stifled when we are controlled by what others think. However, the control that others wield over us is imaginary. It is not empowered by their intentions; it is determined by our beliefs. No one can take control of us—we *give* it away! We give our control in exchange for something else. There is something we feel we can gain, something we value more than having control of our lives. When we value something more than freedom, we will surrender our control of self.

Some people value having a great excuse not to pursue their dreams. Some people value approval. Some people value freedom from responsibility. But anytime we give away our freedom, anytime we feel controlled, we should look to ourselves instead of looking to others and accusing them. We should ask ourselves, "What do I value in this situation so strongly that I am giving up control of my life?" Some people would rather face death than give up their freedoms. It was that very attitude that brought about the American Revolution. "Give me liberty or give me death" was Patrick Henry's cry.

Some people stay in violent relationships because they value financial security more than physical safety. Some people stay in emotionally abusive churches because identifying with a certain group is more important than following God. Make no mistake, anywhere we feel controlled, we have exchanged our freedom for something that we consider to be more valuable.

Trust Jesus rather than Judgments

Jesus came to set us free—free from sin, free from self, free from the law, free from the penalty of sin—free from the power of judgment! Following Him wholeheartedly is the safest life in the world. It has the greatest peace; it has the emotional freedom we all desire. To follow Him wholeheartedly, though, requires that we trust Him enough to apply His truth to our lives. We must walk in love. We must discard our former way of finding safety and happiness and follow His teachings.

One of the most essential areas in which we must trust Him is in giving up the right to judge. The starting point for freeing ourselves from the control of others is releasing others from our own control. It's the law of sowing and reaping. The judgment that we give comes back to us *"pressed down, and shaken together, and running over"* (Luke 6:38). Sometimes that comes in the form of judgment others bring against us; other times it is the way in which the judgments we make of others are measured back to us.

If we judge harshly, we will believe that all people judge harshly. If we attempt to control others through our judgments, we will feel controlled by their judgments. If we gossip about the failures of others, we will think that everyone is gossiping about our failures. The only way to free ourselves from reaping negativity is to sow the seeds of love and mercy. When we do that, we will see some results immediately, while others will take time.

We must release the people in our past and present from our judgment. Paul said, *"Be sure to do what you should, for then you will enjoy the personal satisfaction of having done your work well, and won't need to compare yourself with anyone else"* (Galatians 6:4 NLT). We must come to the place where our sense of approval comes from knowing God, and our sense of confidence from walking with God. We must free ourselves from the attempt to find our superiority through judging others.

We don't know why anyone does anything. Even if we think we do, our judgment does not change reality. It only binds us to the judgments of others. So let's free ourselves by freeing others. Let's give up our vain attempts to control others through our judgments and surrender our right to judge. Only then can we find freedom from the judgment of others.

Seventeen

Overcoming the Need to Judge

✦♋✦

Always accept criticism, but never accept judgment.

As you no doubt have seen by now, judgment has become a crucial part of who we are and how we function in this world. To give up judgment, we must learn an entirely new system of emotional navigation. When we start out on this new journey, we have no idea how much we have been living out of our judgments. Every day we are faced with hundreds of times when we judge people and then act on those judgments. It is amazing how often we assume to know why someone does something.

Do you want to be wise? Deal with only the facts. The moment you stop dealing with facts, you are headed for trouble. You see, our assumptions concerning the motives of others are deadly—both for them and for us. All we can know about anybody is what is observable; that is, what we see or what that person tells us. The Bible teaches us to observe the fruit; it doesn't tell us to take the next step and judge why the person is bringing forth that fruit.

The moment we judge why people do something, instead of dealing with *what* they did, we have crossed the line into judgment. We have entered a place Jesus said not to go. We have infringed upon that which belongs to God alone. Yet it is such a daily occurrence in our lives. It has been ingrained in us since childhood. How many times have we said to our kids, "Why did you do that?" and watched as they immediately got a dazed, far-away look in their eyes and began to explore the unknown possibilities of "why"?

Without realizing it, we are saying, "What you do doesn't really matter as long as your reason is good enough." This is the beginning of a life of self-justification. "If I have a good enough reason, I can get away with anything." Don't ask children *why* they did it. Instead, ask, "What did you do?" They always know what they did. Then ask them, "What do you think you should have done?" Amazingly, they almost always know what they should have done.

From our earliest childhood experiences, we are taught to look for the *why*, instead of the *what*. We are taught to use justification and judgment to negotiate our way out of personal responsibility. This complication is magnified through the fact that we have a sin/fear/self-centered nature. From childhood on, we relate to our world out of our excuses and judgments. All our relationships become an entanglement of our judgments and the judgments of others.

You Can Change You

I don't want to live my life out of my judgment. My judgment isn't that good. Furthermore, I don't want to worry about how I feel about me based on someone else's judgment. I don't want to spend my life on the negative side of "sowing and reaping." Like Paul, I want to learn to live free from others' judgments, and I want to know that you are free from my judgments.

This whole concept of relating to people on the basis of our judgment removes us from the realm of reality, honesty, integrity, responsibility, and accountability. Of course, we can't do anything about what the rest of society is doing, but we can do something about what *we* are doing. We can decide that we will not live our lives based on our judgments. We can choose not to let our lives swing in and out of control based on our judgment of why other people do what they do.

If someone is rude to us, we don't have to imagine, fantasize, and pass judgment. We can either forgive the person or communicate with him. Matthew 18:15 says, *"If your brother sins against you..."* (NIV). Only if a brother actually commits a sin do we have the right to consider it his fault. If we are hypersensitive and our brother has not actually sinned, then the fault is our own. If a brother actually has violated a scriptural principle in relating to us, we should *"show him his fault,"* as verse 15 goes on to say. Most people do not realize when they have offended.

Check Your Heart before You Confront

The problem here is that many people fear confrontation. That fear is usually based on previous negative experiences. If we go to the offender with judgment instead of with the intention of revealing their offense, we always create a conflict. It is essential that we take a new look at the principle of confrontation. The first law of confrontation is this: "Release all judgment." This is not the place to tell the person *why* he did what he did.

You see, judgment seeks a penalty. So if we approach an offender with a heart of judgment, our goal is not to restore the relationship or the person; our goal is to make him suffer, make him see how wrong he is, or make him see how he is what we judged him to be. As Proverbs 15:1 points out, *"A harsh word stirs up anger"* (NIV). Our judgment not only makes the offender angry, but it also makes him defensive. The conflict that results is no longer about the offense. In the face of our judgment, it erupts into a defensive battle about whose judgment is correct.

If we cannot confront in love, we are not ready to confront. We can ask ourselves some questions before we confront in order to check our motives: "Am I doing this just to prove myself right? Am I simply trying to get in the last word? Am I trying to win the argument? Am I trying to get even? Will the way I am doing this promote peace or conflict? Will the way I am planning to handle this negatively affect the person's self-worth?" By asking ourselves these questions, we get a firm grip on our personal responsibilities. The fact that a person has offended us does not relieve us of our personal responsibilities.

Confrontation without Judgment

In a healthy confrontation, we merely reveal to people the effect of their actions. We can point out what they did. We can inform them of how it made us feel. But we can never make it an assessment of their character; we cannot pass judgment. It is completely improper for us to bring up a pattern of this action happening unless we have confronted them in this same manner before. Too often I sit in counseling sessions with people who say, "This person has done this to me for years, and I am sick of it. He is mean and uncaring. He has hurt me for years." I often ask, "How did he respond when you discussed this in the past?" Then, to my utter amazement, I find that they have never discussed it. It is true that the offender should have been sensitive. But if it was not important enough for you to bring it up before now, then you are a partaker in your own pain.

The goal of confrontation must be to help that person as much as to help yourself. You must help him to understand the nature of the offense. He needs to realize the effect his actions have on others so that he can have the opportunity do something about it. If you make confrontation an act of serving people in love, their response will usually be positive and appreciative. Such confrontation could be an opportunity to help them solve a life-dominating problem. Sadly, too often people go through life knowing that they are doing something wrong, but no one ever tells them what it is. Or, when it is addressed, it is done in such anger and judgment that it is unappreciated.

Now, suppose you have made people aware of the effect of their actions. If you confronted them in a positive manner, they are left to deal with how they want to manage their behavior. They can sort out their issues. If the offense occurs again in the future, you can once again tell them how it is affecting you. If it continues unabated, you must realize at some point in time that close involvement with those people is too emotionally costly. They know how their behavior affects you, yet it continues.

We do not know *why* it continues unless they tell us. They may not care how it affects us. They may be attempting to work through personal issues. They may not have taken us seriously. They could be hurting. Or they could actually be attempting to hurt us.

We may not know why they have done nothing about it, but we are free from the control of their actions because we refuse to attach significance to them through our judgment. Now we are on our way to personal freedom and freedom from the judgment of others. We are sowing freedom, and we will reap freedom.

Many times we believe that expressing our judgment in criticism will somehow motivate others to change. It doesn't! It hurts and angers them. When I accept that loving communication will accomplish what I desire, I am free from the need to judge. When I realize how much pain judgment brings, I can begin the process of removing judgment from my life. I learn that it is less painful to ask questions than it is to judge.

We all must realize that our judgments have never brought us peace. They have never helped anyone. Since they have never been of any benefit, then we can consider letting them go.

All people need to be loved. No one needs to be judged. If love does not solve the problem, nothing will. Give up the "right" to judge. Free yourself and the world around you!

Eighteen

Freedom from Justification

The only thing freedom takes away is my excuses!

S o far we have seen that, from our earliest life experiences, we learn to live a reactionary life. Our behavior becomes a reaction to the world around us. Sometimes those reactions are actually based on reality, but they are usually based on our judgments. Reactionary living, regardless of the reason, puts us out of control (in the sense that we are not in charge anymore). In other words, our behavior is no longer based on our choices, but on the actions of others.

When our actions are based on the actions of others; when our decisions are based on someone else's decisions; when our attitudes are based on the attitudes of others, we are out of control. Not only are we out of control, but *the other person* is in control. This type of living makes it impossible for Jesus to be Lord of our lives. He does not have Lordship where He does not have rule, and He does not have rule if He is not the One to whom we respond.

First John 4:8 says, *"He who does not love does not know God, for God is love"* (NKJV). This does not mean the person is not saved. It does not mean a person has never met God as much as it means he or she is not currently experiencing God. People respond to what they are currently experiencing. The only true way to find freedom from judgment is to experience that same freedom that comes from God. God is offering freedom. A refusal to accept the unconditional love of God keeps us from experiencing freedom from judgment.

God's Love Frees You to Stay in Control

We know that fear has to do with judgment. *The Living Bible* addresses the fear of judgment so clearly:

> *We need have no fear of someone who loves us perfectly; his perfect love for us eliminates all dread of what he might do to us. If we are afraid, it is for fear of what he might do to us, and shows that we are not fully convinced that he really loves us.*   (1 John 4:18)

Believing and thereby experiencing this love puts us in a position where we do not react to people, but continually respond to God's love and freedom.

In counseling sessions the world over, we daily hear people say, "I did this because of what she did," "I do this only when he does that," or "Any man would do the same thing if his wife did what she did." People actually look you in the eye, make these kinds of statements, and think they are normal simply because this is how so many people live. Well, guess what? It does not matter if everyone else in the world is doing it. We are still out of control when we react to others.

An intrinsic part of the reactionary life is the need for self-justification. Because our parents always asked us, "Why did you do that?" we developed a concept that says, "If I have a good

103

enough reason, my actions are justified." Even our court systems have fallen into this role. If we have a good enough reason, we can be justified for any crime. Everything in our society has become relative to the judgments of society. The whole world is out of control because of people's insistent claim to the right to judge.

Judgments play a major role in our reactionary living. Because we have no sense of "God in us," we don't feel free to act according to godly principles. Instead, we so crave the acceptance of a warped society that we become controlled by the judgments of that society. Our sense of self-worth comes from the people in our environment instead of from the God who created us. Thus, in order to maintain the approval of others, we feel that we must justify our every decision. The result is that we are forced to continually judge everyone around us, for those judgments become the justifications for our actions.

Good or Bad, It Is Still a Judgment

Contrary to popular opinion, we don't have the right to judge, good or bad. Some people think judgment is wrong only if it causes us to reach a negative point of view. That's not so. We must realize it is just as wrong and destructive to judge someone "good" as it is to judge someone "bad." We often hear people say, "She has a really good heart." We don't know anyone's heart; only God knows a person's heart. People think that a comment like that is a compliment, but, in fact, it is a judgment.

How do these "good judgments" cause negative situations? Let's look at an example. Suppose we go into a business deal with people about whom we have made decisions based on our judgments. We could end up losing money—or fall into some other desperate financial situation—all because we passed a "good" judgment. The Bible says, *"Ye shall know them by their fruits"* (Matthew 7:16). All we can really know about other people is their track record. Everything else is a judgment. The Christian world is full of people who have lost fortunes because they judged people to be good or trustworthy apart from their track record.

We all should learn to hear and follow the Spirit of God as He leads. Too often, however, this becomes a spiritual excuse for judgment. So many times someone makes a decision on the basis of a judgment like, "I think he has a good heart," or "I really feel good about doing business with her." Then the person loses his life savings or has a terrible business or relational experience. Sadly, in the end, he usually becomes angry with God, as if He had misled him. In Proverbs 19:3, *The Living Bible* says, *"A man may ruin his chances by his own foolishness and then blame it on the Lord!"*

All such feelings of good or bad are subjective. They may be the voice of God; they may not. But if something is the voice of God, it will stand the scrutiny of discovery. It is not a denial of faith to check someone's job or credit references. It is not an insult to the individual to make sure his or her story and references are valid. We are not calling a person a liar by checking for concrete data; we are simply being wise stewards. We must always remember that the Holy Spirit will not lead us to violate the wisdom of God.

It seems that when we want to do something with people, we have to pass a judgment in their favor; or when we don't want to do something with people, we pass a judgment against them. The key question to ask ourselves is this: "Why do I need to justify my behavior with a judgment?" Even if, after we have checked references, we do not feel comfortable hiring a person, we do not have to find fault in that individual to justify our action. It should be enough that we are not comfortable. That does not mean he or she is a bad person; it just means we are not comfortable.

You Can Be Kind and Still Say "No"

Many times people have come to me in concern because I am treating someone else in a kind manner. They feel that they need to inform me about the person's past. Sometimes that is actually helpful, but more often than not it seems that people think, "If you know about this person, you will not be kind to them." In other words, they think kindness must be justified.

In Jesus, we have been made free. We are freed from sin, judgment, and hell. We are freed from thousands of things. But just as important as all other freedoms is our freedom from this world's system. We don't have to work the same system everyone else works. We are citizens of the kingdom of God. The motivating principle that sets us free is love. Only when God's love motivates everything we do will we actually experience freedom from judgment.

Sometimes we place so much emphasis on what we are free from that we forget what we are now free to do. More than anything else, we are free to give unconditional, unearned love. Actually, we now owe a debt of love—but we don't owe it to people. We owe it to God. We give love back to God by giving people the same degree of love God has given us. Unconditional love is the only debt we incurred from the cross of Christ. All others were paid.

We can fulfill others' requests or deny their requests and still walk in love toward them. How? Look at the characteristics of God's love found in 1 Corinthians 13:4–7:

> *Love is patient, love is kind. It does not envy, it does not boast, it is not proud. It is not rude, it is not self-seeking, it is not easily angered, it keeps no record of wrongs. Love does not delight in evil but rejoices with the truth. It always protects, always trusts, always hopes, always perseveres.* (NIV)

These are not attitudes that we display because we judge people to be worthy. These are what we should display because we are in Jesus. How we treat people should have nothing to do with who we think they are. It should have everything to do with who we are in Jesus. Even if we are refusing to give them a job, make them a loan, or fulfill a favor, we can still relate to them with these attributes. We do not need to justify our kindness.

Too often we fear that walking in love will make us too vulnerable. We tend to view love as a "doormat" syndrome. We think that if we walk in love, others will walk all over us. But love cannot be manipulated; it cannot be controlled; it cannot be taken advantage of. Jesus walked in love at all times, yet He was never controlled or manipulated, and He never felt compelled to fulfill everyone's requests.

The realization that you are still walking in love, even though you are not giving in to another's request, frees you from the control of the judgment of others. Their judgments are no longer the standard that determines your life. God's Word and Jesus' example are your standard instead. When you are free from the need to justify your actions through your judgments, you are free to say "no" in the kindest way! And you don't need any excuses!

Nineteen

Freedom from Self-Judgment

❦

You have the right to judge only if you are smarter than God.

O f all the pain-producing, destructive aspects of judgment, self-judgment is the worst. Why? Self-judgment becomes the basis for our self-talk. Negative self-talk, coupled with the strong emotion it can produce, will write all manner of destructive things on our hearts. In the end, self-judgment usually becomes a condemnation or a justification—and neither is healthy.

Paul said, in his first letter to the Corinthians, that it really didn't matter to him how others judged him. He gave us some insight into his freedom from the judgment of others:

> *But with me it is a very small thing that I should be judged by you or by a human court. In fact, I do not even judge myself. For I know of nothing against myself, yet I am not justified by this; but He who judges me is the Lord. Therefore judge nothing before the time, until the Lord comes, who will both bring to light the hidden things of*

108

darkness and reveal the counsels of the hearts. Then each one's praise will come from God.

(1 Corinthians 4:3–5 NKJV)

Paul's freedom from the judgment of others was linked to his freedom from self-judgment.

Don't Even Judge Yourself

In the original language, *"I know of nothing against myself"* indicates that Paul did not know or see himself clearly. That is the problem with self-judgment. Our perception is always clouded, so when we do pass a judgment, we do not know if it is accurate. So he continued, "Don't judge anything before the time. I don't even judge myself."

Paul did not assume himself to be right or wrong. He didn't use self-judgment as an excuse to defend or condemn himself. Paul simply attempted to follow God wholeheartedly and walk in love. His sense of identity came from his relationship with Jesus, not from his self-evaluation. He earnestly sought to follow God and keep a clear conscience. Because he was free from "works-righteousness" (trying to earn righteousness by what we do), he did not need the constant validation that comes from self-evaluation. He knew he was righteous in Jesus; that was the source of his peace.

This concept is foreign to current Christian thinking. We are so trapped in works-righteousness that we endlessly inventory our works, both good and bad. We keep a performance score-card, and we judge ourselves from that scorecard. Then, because we use judgment as a standard of self-approval, we become subject to everyone else's judgment as well. Thus we cannot free ourselves from the control of the judgment of others until we free ourselves from the control of self-judgment.

When Jesus said, "Don't judge," He meant it. We must not judge others, and we must not judge ourselves. As we will see in subsequent chapters, self-judgment causes emotional dysfunction, physical sickness, and even death. I don't want my life to be controlled by the judgment of others or of myself. I know of no one other than Jesus whom I would trust with such a powerful, life-altering responsibility. We must commit to a life free from judgment. Releasing our judgments about ourselves not only frees us from the judgments of others, but it is also key in freeing us from the need to judge others.

There is, of course, a place for healthy self-evaluation. (We will discuss this in later chapters.) This self-evaluation, however, does not reach life-controlling judgments that alter our ability to function. On the other hand, when we are in pain or sin, we are emotionally blinded. We see and interpret events through a veil of subjective distortion. As a result, our conscience causes us to either condemn or justify. There is simply no safe way to reach self-judgment.

The Problem with Fixing Myself

The parable of the wheat and the tares contains a principle that applies to self-judgment.

> *Another parable He put forth to them, saying: "The kingdom of heaven is like a man who sowed good seed in his field; but while men slept, his enemy came and sowed tares among the wheat and went his way. But when the grain had sprouted and produced a crop, then the tares also appeared. So the servants of the owner came and said to him, 'Sir, did you not sow good seed in your field? How then does it have tares?' He said to them, 'An enemy has done this.' The servants said to him, 'Do you want us then to go and gather them up?' But he said, 'No, lest while you gather up the tares you also uproot the wheat with them.'"*
> (Matthew 13:24–29 NKJV)

Any attempt to dig out the tares before the appointed time will result in destroying the wheat. You see, wheat and tares look identical until they bear fruit. In the same way, anytime we get into the "I'm going to fix it" mode, we usually do as much damage as good. So we should not worry about trying to fix ourselves. We must simply follow the Holy Spirit as He leads us through life. Getting healed and being made whole are serendipitous. It is not the goal of the journey, but it is a wonderful part of the process.

Few people know why they do what they do. Introspection is such a subjective process that we seldom reach the right conclusions. If I am hurting or in pain, it is doubtful that I can see clearly enough to get to the real root of my problem. That would be tantamount to allowing a mentally disturbed patient evaluate and diagnose his own problems. The treatment is then no better than the diagnosis. When hurting people use self-diagnosis, the self-prescribed treatment is often the source of additional pain.

Simply Accept God's View

Self-judgment actually may be the very root through which all other forms of perverted judgment flourish in our lives. We must discard our self-view and live out of our new identity in Jesus, thereby freeing ourselves from the faulty judgments of others as well as those of our own deceived hearts. We must accept God's view and opinion of us and reject all others. Any other view, from any other source, will produce dysfunction and pain. God says we are loved; we are righteous; we are accepted; we are anointed. More than two hundred times in the New Testament, God tells us our identity.

For example, Romans 6:11 says, *"So you should consider yourselves dead to sin and able to live for the glory of God through Christ Jesus"* (NLT). Why should we consider ourselves to be this way? Simple! This is how God sees us, and that's the way it is.

"Yes, but I have all sorts of problems. This can't be true about me." That's the problem. You don't consider God's opinion to be real; therefore, you will never experience His version of reality. You will experience only what you consider to be true. When you consider this verse to be true, you will be free from all other judgments regarding it, including your own.

The only judgment you must now accept is the judgment of God. Your old man, with the sin nature, was judged guilty and has been crucified with Christ. Your new man is raised up in righteousness in Christ. You are a new creation. You must accept God's judgment and live out of that judgment. To be controlled by any other judgment is to usurp the Lordship of Jesus in your life.

God judges you to be free from the effects and the penalties of sin. He judges that you are righteous in Jesus; therefore, you are qualified for all He has promised to anyone who believes. Will you surrender your view for His? Will you exchange your judgment for His? Starting today, never say to or about yourself that which is not consistent with what God says about you in Jesus!

Twenty

Knowing
My Stuff

·❧❧·

I don't need to carry your pain. I have enough of my own.

It seems that we constantly, albeit with good intentions, invade emotional territory that is not ours. We would much rather take on other people's issues than deal with our own. Invading others' issues is obviously wrong. Many times people invite us into these areas, but we seldom stop at the biblical bounds of ministry. We have crossed boundaries when we take on the emotional weight of their problems.

Even though our concepts of ministry, or of helping others, are the accepted norm, they are often contrary to biblical principles. We cross lines with little awareness of scriptural or emotional violation. We create conflicts and invade privacy, then wonder why we have chaos and pain. The Bible says, *"So don't worry about tomorrow, for tomorrow will bring its own worries"* (Matthew 6:34 NLT). That principle applies across the board. I don't need to carry your pain. I have enough of my own.

How Did We Get into This?

Sometimes we unconsciously take on other people's problems as a way to escape our own. Research indicates that our minds must, for survival purposes, create distractions from the problems we are afraid to face. Obviously, that denial does not reduce the pain in our lives; it just keeps us from facing what we believe to be too painful. For some the acceptable alternative is to overwork; for some it is sickness; others need a crisis; and for still others, the way to avoid pain is to take on other people's issues.

Our lack of emotional sensitivity with others is a mere reflection of the absence of personal awareness. We cross boundaries because we are unaware. We are unaware because we are in denial. And we are in denial because we are afraid to face our own pain. In short, we must get in touch with ourselves before we can know the difference between our issues and those of others.

In 1981 I left the pulpit for about a year. I really had no intention of ever going back into the ministry, and I never would have returned except for one thing: God spoke to my heart and said, "Son, you try to do for people what even I won't do for them."

At that point, I reread the Gospels. I read them with an open mind, approaching them as if I had never read them before. I took nothing for granted. I assumed to know nothing. I questioned everything that I thought I knew. What I discovered was absolutely life-changing. I saw how Jesus related to and interacted with people. It was amazing how many scenarios presented Him with the opportunity to "cross the line." He refused, however, to be drawn into someone else's stuff. He never invaded another person's boundaries, and He never did for people what they should do for themselves.

Don't Be a Fool

In the story of the Prodigal Son, the father is rather well-off. Nevertheless, the son departs. Then the son begins a process in which he must learn to face the consequences of his actions. The book of Proverbs tells us that a fool is a person who will not be taught by instruction (Proverbs 15:5). This is not the word for "fool" as it is in Matthew 5, where it means a person who is worthless and of no value. A fool, from this perspective, is a person who will not learn by instruction; instead, he or she chooses to learn the hard way—by experience.

The Bible says that stripes are for the back of a fool. (See Proverbs 17:10; 29:19.) A fool's only hope of learning is when he has faced the consequences of his actions. Much of the pain in our lives comes simply because we will not listen. Children who do not listen to their parents usually experience a lot of pain. People who do not seek and consider good advice always end up in trouble. They want to avoid pain, but they want to do things their own way. The most tragic person is the one who refuses advice, experiences pain, yet still refuses to learn from the consequences. Such people are doomed to a life of pain. There is no deliverance for the person who chooses to live the life of foolishness.

The greater fool is the one who tries to keep a fool from paying the price. Many times when my children and others in my life were going in the wrong direction, I offered wise advice or help, and they continued going in the wrong direction. Eventually they got into hardship. At that point, humanistic attitudes would make me feel that I was obligated to rescue them. However, to do so would violate everything the Scriptures taught me about wisdom and relationships. Too many times, though, I intervened so they would not suffer the consequences of their actions and choices. Then I wondered why they never grew up in that area.

Let Consequences Teach

Is it their problem? No, it's my problem. When I crossed their personal boundaries, I made their problem into my problem. I refused to allow them to go through a process in which they had to face the consequences of their actions and thereby learn. I prevented them from taking the only real opportunity they had to learn. I bailed them out.

Let's go back to the story of the Prodigal Son. The prodigal's father had the resources to bail him out, but he didn't. It wasn't until the son was eating pig food as a slave (he was paying the price) that he came to himself. Hardship has a way of getting us in touch with reality! Consequences are sobering! When people face their consequences, free from our intervention, they turn to God. Then He has the opportunity to become their Teacher.

People learn through consequences. We call it love when we intervene, make decisions for them, and get in the middle of their stuff. But love is based on truth. When we violate scriptural principles, it is not love.

Judgment would cause us to say, "I made bad decisions, and God is now teaching me a lesson by making me suffer." This type of thinking is a continuation of foolishness. It is still a denial that these consequences are the direct result of my actions and that God has nothing to do with it. Of course, God is always there to lead us out, but He is never the one who put us in the pain. Rather, He always stands ready to help when we are ready to receive help—but He never forces His help on us.

Let People Go

As he was starting out on a trip, a man came running to him and knelt down and asked, "Good Teacher, what must I do to get to heaven?" "Why do you call me good?" Jesus asked. "Only God is truly good! But as for your question—you know the commandments: don't kill, don't commit adultery, don't steal, don't lie, don't cheat, respect your father and mother." "Teacher," the man replied, "I've never once broken a single one of those laws." Jesus felt genuine love for this man as he looked at him. "You lack only one thing," he told him; "go and sell all you have and give the money to the poor—and you shall have treasure in heaven—and come, follow me." Then the man's face fell, and he went sadly away, for he was very rich. Jesus watched him go, then turned around and said to his disciples, "It's almost impossible for the rich to get into the Kingdom of God!" (Mark 10:17-23 TLB)

When the man walked away, Jesus didn't stop him. He accepted where the man was and recognized that he had issues he needed to resolve with God. If the man didn't resolve those issues, it wouldn't matter if Jesus negotiated him back into the fold, for eventually that would not be enough. Jesus recognized and accepted that the young man had some stuff that he had to work out. If Jesus had pursued him, it would have become Jesus' stuff. We, on the other hand, pursue people and negotiate terms—albeit for our benefit, not theirs.

We pursue people and situations that we shouldn't, and when things don't come out the way we want them to, we say, "You're making me unhappy," or "You are hurting me." The truth is that we're not happy because we made other people's stuff ours. We are experiencing the pain of their foolishness because we crossed a boundary that we should not have crossed.

We can never minister to people whom we judge. The moment we judge, we pronounce a sentence. That sentence may be repentance, or it may be punishment; but whether good or bad, we are now following our own agenda. Now how they respond is about us. We have emotionally factored ourselves into the equation of their lives. We now need for them to act according to our judgment. If they don't, it is a violation against us.

We must learn to let people go to God and deal with their own issues in their own time. God is much more effective at dealing with people's stuff than we are! If we give people the truth in love, then leave them alone, the Holy Spirit can do more in their lives than our manipulation and pressure can do. The problem is that we aren't in touch with our own hearts or God in our hearts. We are so accustomed to living life out of our judgments that we don't know where we stop and someone else starts. We don't know the difference between their issues and our issues.

Know Who You Are in God

I was astonished as I reread the Gospels and saw how Jesus related to people. When Jesus and His mother were at a wedding, she mentioned to Him that the hosts were out of wine. He said, in effect, "What does that have to do with Me?" (See John 2:1–4.) On another occasion, when His mother and brothers thought He was crazy, they came to take Him home. "Your mother is here to see You," people in the crowd reported. He replied, "Let Me tell you who My mother and brothers are." (See Matthew 12:46–50.) In one case, someone came and tried to draw Him into a dispute about an inheritance. He simply said, "Who made Me your judge?" (See Luke 12:14.) At first these answers might seem cold, but they aren't. Jesus simply wouldn't let people draw Him into their stuff. He wouldn't let people bring Him into the issues they had to solve in their own hearts.

Jesus knew where He was going. He knew who He was. His identity and self-worth were established because of who He was in relationship to God. Therefore, people could not draw Him into all their personal or religious issues. We, on the other hand, get drawn into these issues because we don't know who we are in Jesus. We lack a biblically based sense of self-worth. We're not confident in the love and acceptance of God, so we try to get it from people. This need-oriented behavior always puts us in their stuff.

We don't want conflict, and we want to be liked, so we are drawn into things that are not ours. Yet they become conflicts.

We make commitments that we don't really want, and then we get frustrated with others because we think they are using and manipulating us. (It is amazing that we can't say "no" and still feel good about ourselves.) We don't have enough peace, joy, or fulfillment in our own hearts, so we think that if we can somehow satisfy everyone else, they will like us, and that will meet our need. But that doesn't happen.

Why do we let others draw us into their stuff? Why do we have to be what someone else wants us to be? What's wrong with us that we can't love others the way they are? Why do we have to make others into the people we want them to be before we can love them? Why do they have to believe the same things we do before we can love them? Why do we have to be who others want us to be before we can believe that they will love us?

If your sense of being loved and accepted is not rooted in your relationship with God, you will make yourself subject to others' judgments. You will lack the emotional freedom to allow others to process their own issues with God. If your need for the approval of others supersedes what you know to be biblical wisdom, then you will end up entangling your life with their issues, making them your own.

Let me give you some handy advice: Just say "no."

Twenty-one

Judging God

❧

We have judged God and found Him guilty of those things we do not understand.

T he Word of God clearly commands, *"You shall not make for yourself an idol in the form of anything in heaven above"* (Exodus 20:4 NIV). There is not a Christian alive who would knowingly breach this command. The very idea appalls us. Yet, in the most subtle and seductive manner, we all are guilty of idolatry to some degree. We do not commit idolatry by going into the woods, cutting down a tree, fashioning it into an image, and bowing before it. No one would dare such an insult to God. Nevertheless, we are just as guilty of creating idols as any other generation.

We do not create our idols with an ax and carpenter's tools, but with our vain imaginations.

> *For the weapons of our warfare are not carnal, but mighty through God to the pulling down of strong holds; casting down imaginations, and every high thing that exalteth itself against the knowledge of God, and bringing into captivity every thought to the obedience of Christ.*
>
> (2 Corinthians 10:4–5)

Our vain imagination becomes a "high thing" that opposes all that we know about God through His Word and through the life of Jesus. To be blunt, we create idolatrous concepts of God when we pass judgment on Him.

We Judge God because We Don't Believe What He Says

The children of Israel judged God and found Him guilty.

> *Therefore, as the Holy Spirit says: "Today, if you will hear His voice, do not harden your hearts as in the rebellion, in the day of trial in the wilderness, where your fathers tested Me, tried Me, and saw My works forty years."*
>
> (Hebrews 3:7–9 NKJV)

While in the wilderness, the children of Israel put God on trial and found Him guilty of lying. They judged Him as unable to bring them into the land of Canaan as He had promised. For forty years they tested God—that is, they kept Him on trial—because they did not consider Him able or willing to do what He said.

The truth is, they *knew* God was able. They had seen all His works as they had come out of Egypt. They had seen Pharaoh and his armies defeated. They had seen the miracle of the Red Sea parting. They had experienced enough miraculous phenomena with God that they should have had no problem believing His promise. The fact of the matter is that they really didn't trust themselves. Like us, they had no problem believing in the mighty power of God. The Israelites believed His every promise—until it had to be done through them.

"I have given you the land; go up and drive out the inhabitants," seems like a contradictory message. Yet that is exactly what God said to them. *"And Joshua said unto the children of Israel, How long are ye slack to go to possess the land, which the LORD God of your fathers hath given you?"* (Joshua 18:3). They trusted God's power until they had to trust it to work through them.

You see, we attempt to recreate God in our own image. Instead of opening our minds and hearts to see things the way God shows them to us, we want to make God see things the way we show them to Him. The word *imaginations* in 2 Corinthians 10 comes from the Greek word *logos*. Logos has to do with logic, reasoning, or computation. (See *Strong's Concordance*, #G3056.) The *New King James Version* translates it as "arguments." A vain imagination is the result of reasoning, computing, and reaching a concept about God that is not based on truth or reality. It is an argument with reality.

We Judge God in Order to Justify Ourselves

We create these idolatrous images of God in many ways. The first and most obvious method is—being so self-centered—when we interpret the world and all that is in it based on our perception of ourselves. God created man in His own image, but as god of our own world we recreate God to fit into our perception of the world. We create a concept of God that justifies our life experiences.

When we begin to ask "why" in regard to God, we enter into judgment about Him. God has told us all we need to know about Him in His Word. He sent Jesus, who modeled all that He is. We should be able to look at the life of Jesus and understand God. But we don't—we look to our experiences and ask, "Why did this happen to me?" Or we look at the tragedies of the world and ask, "Why did God let that happen?"

When we answer those questions, we become like the builder of idols. Each idea, each false concept, carves and shapes an image of the god we come to believe in. Thus we create a god that justifies our perception of the world.

Like the children of Israel, we put God on trial and find Him guilty of negligence toward all mankind. He is condemned for allowing the injustice of the world. He is found guilty for not rescuing every child who has been hurt or abused. He is found guilty of allowing hearts to be broken.

After Job spent nearly forty chapters blaming God for his troubles, God asked him a question. *"Would you condemn Me that you may be justified?"* (Job 40:8 NKJV). The answer for Job and the human race is an overwhelming "Yes! We would gladly accuse You, God, to justify ourselves." We attest to that when at nearly every Christian funeral someone quotes, "The Lord giveth and the Lord taketh away." (See Job 1:21.) We somehow fail to understand that that passage was a part of Job's ramblings. We fail to see that Job had held himself out as innocent, without responsibility in all his trouble. Sure, he was a righteous man, but he still had responsibilities.

God Is Good

We even judge God in our testimonies. I remember listening to one of my favorite preachers as I was driving to college one morning. He told a story of getting healed and then explained how he got God to do it. I was intrigued by his testimony. It was so powerful. As I sat in my car before class listening to his story, the Lord spoke to my heart and said, "That's not why I healed him." As in most testimonies, the *why* was subjective, assumptive reasoning that glorified the man's faith instead of the goodness of God.

It is an amazing thing that in all our testimonies about God's goodness, in the end the reason why God does His miraculous deeds is because of something we do. We elevate works and legalism. We make needy listeners feel that they have just not yet done something as great as we did. We create an image of God that is totally inconsistent with all that Jesus modeled to us. We lead people to bow down to an idol of dead works and performance.

God does what He does because of the finished work of Jesus. He is a loving Father who has made a way for us to be delivered from hurt and pain. Anything else that attempts to say *why* is a faulty judgment that creates a false image of God.

The pain we bring to our lives because of our judgments about people is nominal compared to the devastation that comes when we assume that God is responsible for tragedy and then judge why He did what we have accused Him of doing. Once we have formed judgments against God, we have no hiding place from life's storms. We have nowhere to run in the time of trouble.

The two most important judgments you can ever make are how you see yourself and how you see God. The two are overlapping realities. They are a continuum; they are so interconnected that one forges the other. I cannot see myself properly until I see God properly. Only after I accept Jesus' testimony of who God is can I see who I am in relationship to Him. My concept of self can never evolve independently of my concept of God. After all, I am created in the likeness and image of God. I am a new creation in Christ.

Every time I create a concept of God to justify or explain what I do not understand, I alter my perception of God, which ultimately alters my perception of myself. A downward spiral of one begins a downward spiral of the other. Paul said, "Don't judge anything before its time." (See 1 Corinthians 4:5.) So any perception or belief about God that is inconsistent with what Jesus showed us through His life and teaching must be rejected. Anything that we cannot reconcile, we must leave alone.

We all have unanswered questions about God and life. We all have situations that are beyond our explanation. However, we must not let our need for judgment cause us to judge God. The end of that path is devastation. Accept the testimony that Jesus modeled of God. Believe who He is. When you do not understand, do not judge!

Twenty-two

Associations and Judgments

✦✦✦

When we make this equal that, we are in judgment.

M emories are a powerful tool that can work for us or against us. God taught the children of Israel to use certain methods to stimulate memories. For example, they were to stack a bunch of rocks at certain places. When their children asked why the rocks were there, the parents were to tell a story about God's deliverance. Eventually, every time the children looked at the stack of rocks, they would think about God's ability to deliver. In short, He taught them to make an association—to connect one thing with another.

Although association can be a very powerful tool for good, it also can work against us. We tend to associate certain activities, events, words, or even behavior types with past experiences. This is a form of stereotyping. Because of associations that we have made, we tend to stereotype others based on their speech, skin color, position of authority, or any number of different factors.

Before we reach school age—while still very young in life—we have created a complex maze of associations whereby we judge the world around us for years to come. We can feel very distrustful of someone and never realize that it is simply a matter of an association. If someone in our past violated our trust and that person had a particular trait, then, chances are, when we meet another person with that trait, we will withhold trust and never really know why.

This is a form of subconscious judgment. Love does not prejudge; love allows people's character to emerge. Though it does not naively give its trust to everyone, it does not withhold trust on the basis of associations. When we find ourselves relating to someone in a way that violates the principles of love, we must deal with the underlying issue in our hearts. Even if nine out of ten people with a particular trait take advantage of us, that does not give us the right to judge the tenth one.

You Can Be Wise without Judging

Proverbs 12:26 says, *"A righteous man is cautious in friendship"* (NIV). It is wise to be cautious in all relationships; however, we should never allow that caution to cross over into judgment. It is healthy for us to recognize that people with a particular behavioral pattern tend to do certain things in certain situations. Yet we can never *judge* that they will do a certain thing. We can observe or realize that their particular track record says we cannot trust them in that area. But we cannot judge by saying that because they have this particular behavior pattern, they will do a specific thing, or that because other people who are similar to them do this, they will, too.

There is an old proverb that says, "Caution is the parent of safety." It seems that in our inability to walk in equity, we tend to go from one extreme to the other. Either we trust no one, or we trust everyone. Proverbs also says, *"The wise look ahead to see what is coming, but fools deceive themselves....The wise are cautious and avoid danger; fools plunge ahead with great confidence"* (Proverbs 14:8, 16 NLT).

It is wise not to venture in trust beyond what we know about a person. It is, however, wicked to hold him or her in suspicion without reason. If we start down a dark street and see a group of young, unshaven men with spiked hair, chains hanging off their clothes, and arms covered in tattoos coming up the street, we had better consider taking another route. But we have no reason to say that all those young men are violent people. Proverbs 27:12 in *The Living Bible* says, *"A sensible man watches for problems ahead and prepares to meet them. The simpleton never looks, and suffers the consequences."*

Even when people's track records say that they should not be trusted in an area, we still do not know if they are being honest this time. We do not refuse to trust them because their past *proves* they are currently dishonest; rather, we have the right to refuse to do business with them because their past makes us feel uncomfortable trusting them. Their past says it is *probable* that they are not trustworthy today. Wisdom and love give us the freedom to take appropriate actions without having to pass a judgment.

Consider the Association before You Judge

Associations become judgments the moment we say, "This equals that." Regardless of the similarities, the past does not necessarily equal the future. We cannot judge one person on the basis of other people's actions. When people come to my church from abusive churches, I always ask of them, "Don't punish me for what the people in your past have done. Give me the benefit of the doubt until I give you reason to do otherwise."

When we allow associations to dominate our emotions, we give control of our lives to those people from the past who hurt us. We are, through our current judgments, allowing their actions to determine our future happiness. When things seem similar, it is always safe to ask questions. If questions are not allowed, then prudence would imply that this is not an area in which we should trust, but we still do not know *why.*

When someone does something that causes past suspicions to arise, we must refuse to give in to judgment. Francis Bacon, a British philosopher, essayist, and statesman of the late 1500s and early 1600s, said, "There is nothing which makes a man suspect much more than to know little, and, therefore, men should remedy suspicion by procuring to know more and not keep their suspicions in smother." Information is the key to conquering suspicion. If we are afraid to gather that information, then we must realize that it is *our* problem and not precipitously project that fear onto others.

Many of our associations are a matter of semantics. In a controlling church, the use of the word *authority* may refer to people being forced to follow the direction of the elders. When I use the word *authority,* it is a reference to the authority of God's Word. In one environment, the word *submit* may mean obedience; in another, it may mean a yielding attitude. Many cults use the same terminology as Christians. Therefore, you cannot judge on the basis of semblance. If something bothers you, then without attacking or appearing emotionally distressed, simply ask, "What do you mean when you use this terminology?"

When associations cause our emotions to spin out of control, we are being dominated by something that does not exist. We are being angered, threatened, or hurt by that which has no being. We are controlled by what "I think you think." All we need to do to free ourselves from phantom control is to ask questions. Then, whether our suspicions are correct or incorrect, we have saved ourselves from a painful experience because we refused to judge.

Twenty-three

Spiritual Gifts and Judgment

❧

"Thus saith the Lord" is an inarguable position!

As I walked through the door of the modern yet unkempt home, an attractive, dark-haired young woman nervously greeted me. Her eyes avoided mine as if she were afraid I would see something she sought to keep hidden. As we walked to the kitchen table, which was the center of activity in her home, her hands fidgeted, secretly betraying her fear. When we sat down at the table, she lost her composure. Her fear and desperation flooded out like a single stream of lava from a volcanic explosion. Her words were like red-hot rocks that burned on impact.

"Why?" she shouted. "Why would God make me do something like this?"

After calming the distraught woman enough to conduct rational communication, I queried, "What is it you think God is asking you to do?"

"Tonight, Brother Bill came over and prophesied that it was the will of God for me to marry him, and I don't want to marry him!"

I spent the rest of the evening persuading this angry woman that God had not spoken through the mouth of this spiritual manipulator. As unreasonable as this scenario seems, every day people are affected and controlled by the actions, judgments, and influence of others because of the elevated position they have given those people in their minds.

Having Spiritual Gifts Does Not Give You License

In a day when so many people claim to speak in the name of God, those who desperately seek to follow God are easily controlled by the judgments of spiritual leaders. This lady had seen this man minister in a way that made her believe he spoke for God all the time, so she assumed that this "prophecy" must be true as well.

We need to realize that the presence of spiritual gifts (such as those listed in 1 Corinthians 12) does not equal the presence of godly character. The Bible is full of people whom God used mightily, even though they had serious character flaws. Neither does having spiritual gifts give any person the right to overstep the boundaries of our lives. God Himself does not exert the kind of control that many "spiritually minded" people attempt to exert. Spiritual gifts do not come because we are holier than someone else is; they usually come because we are more willing and available. If we could earn them, then they wouldn't be gifts.

A valid question I am often asked when talking about these things is this: "What about the prophetic gifts?" For years, certain circles have placed great emphasis on the "revelation gifts" like discerning of spirits and prophecy. These are legitimate spiritual gifts. But the way these gifts have been presented to the body of Christ is a perversion of biblical principle. There is no gift from God that makes us able to look into the heart of another person. There is no gift that reveals to us the motives of another like we think prophecy can. The Bible specifically explains the purpose of New Testament prophecy: *"But he who prophesies speaks edification and exhortation and comfort to men"* (1 Corinthians 14:3 NKJV).

The fact that one might see something wrong in another's life is not a spiritual gift. We all can look at each other and see things that might not be right—that is not a gift! That can be the wise fruit of life experiences, or sometimes it can simply be a critical attitude. The gift is when we can see the unacceptable and still allow something to come forth in our lives to edify, exhort, and comfort the person. It isn't "discerning of spirits" to judge people and then get into their stuff to try to fix them. We have already discussed how dangerous it is to try to fix someone! As we saw from the parable of the wheat and the tares, we should not try to pull the tares out of a person's life. When we try to fix someone by pulling up the tares, in the process we also could pull up the wheat. I have seen a lot people who did not survive the church's "fixing" them. I was almost one of them. It is not ministry to attack what is wrong; it is ministry to offer people the help that will give them a new life. Ministry is about where we are going, not where we have been.

Can You Love "in Spite Of"?

Not long after a man began to attend my church, he became a suspect in a violent murder case. When it all started coming out in the media, people asked me what I was going to do about the situation. I said, "I'm going to love him." "How can you love somebody like that?" was the usual question. "The same way I love you," was my standard answer. Can we justify the crime because he had a terrible childhood? No, he had a normal childhood. Was he defending himself? No, he was just a jealous, controlling, abusive boyfriend who killed a helpless girl. There was no way for anyone to justify his crime.

In these situations, we start looking for ways to justify our actions. Too often our approach is, "We can love you if we can give you an excuse." We can give an excuse, however, only if we can answer the question "why" in an acceptable manner. In other words, we are so bound by judgment that we need a judgment to justify our kindness to others. Judgment that gives us permission to be kind is nearly always a factor in denial. "If I can't love him without justification, then I am the one who has a problem." The fact that God loves people should be enough.

I have always been a streetwise person because I was on the street at a young age. I can easily spot a scam before others can. That is not a gift. The fact that I can spot a con artist, liar, or someone who is playing games has caused me many problems. People told me that the insight I had was a gift, but the truth was that I had just "been around." I was very critical and cynical. Until I allowed God to work in my life and help me to love such people with all their faults, I was miserable. I saw people's faults, but instead of being compelled to help them, I was compelled to criticize them.

We must commit ourselves to a life of love. When we see faults in others, we must show them the kindness of God that makes them feel safe in owning and conquering their problem. Extending love to the young man who had committed murder gave him the courage to turn himself in and confess his crime. Before anyone knew whether he was innocent or guilty, I told him from the pulpit, "If you are guilty, you may go to the electric chair, but God will still love you. If you are guilty, we will still love you. If you are guilty and this costs you your life, that will not be the end. There is life after death. If you have made a commitment to Jesus, He will accept you into eternity with peace. We will never justify your crime, but we will love you and stand with you until the end." The next day, he turned himself in and confessed. He has remained a friend since then.

My effectiveness in ministry today has been a result of my ability to see through the games people play, yet still love them. More than once I have sat down with people and very lovingly said, "I think this is the game you are playing. I want you to know I still love you, but I'm not going to buy into your game."

On the other hand, when people succeed in deceiving us, our unwitting love and acceptance means nothing to them. As a matter of fact, they will despise us for it. But when they realize that we see them as they are and still love them anyway, their heart will be touched. We are showing them the character of God. *That* is a gift!

Leaders Should Not Usurp the Holy Spirit's Job

Because leaders speak for God from the pulpit, they often wrongly think that they have the right to speak for God in every area. When they tag the end of their conversation with, "The Lord said," or "In the name of the Lord," or "God showed me," it becomes inarguable. When we attribute people's words to God, their judgment will completely control us. After all, who can stand against God?

We all should hear from God for ourselves. God put His Spirit in us so we would not have to go to others to seek Him. He is alive in us. When we have daily, personal involvement with Him, no one can ever lead us by spiritual manipulation. The apostle John faced this issue of spiritual control with the agnostics of his day. In the epistle of 1 John, he had to free the people from the idea that there were some who had special anointing. Those who claimed this special anointing also claimed the right to control the lives of others. John's readers were being seduced by the judgments of others. And because they held these "special" people in unrealistic esteem, they were self-deceived.

We all are just children and servants of God. Although some of us may be leaders, that does not give us any special rights or privileges in the lives of others. We can serve them, but we cannot be a substitute for the Holy Spirit in their lives. When we cross people's boundaries and attempt to control them, we are no longer serving them. We can submit thoughts, ideas, teaching, and even prophecy to them; but, in the end, people must direct their lives out of their own relationship with God.

When we feel controlled by a spiritual leader, we must not judge his or her motive, but simply realize that we have given that leader too much influence in our own hearts. That is our stuff, regardless of the leader's intent. At that point, we must give that place in our lives back to its rightful Owner, Jesus our Lord, who faced sin and death for us. Only He has the right to direct our lives!

Twenty-four

A Word for the Clueless

❦

Listen when your enemies criticize you. They'll tell you the truth that your friends avoid.

For some, the word *judgment* is a red flag they wave every time they face scrutiny. It is the defense mechanism of the foolish. It is the cry of the victim. It is the means whereby those who lack understanding are able to avoid any form of criticism. "You are judging me!" may be the ultimate defense.

Proverbs says, *"If you listen to constructive criticism, you will be at home among the wise. If you reject criticism, you only harm yourself; but if you listen to correction, you grow in understanding"* (Proverbs 15:31–32 NLT). No criticism is pleasant. There is not a person in the world who does not have to put forth extra effort in order to respond positively to criticism.

Some wise and patient souls are able to accept criticism when it comes from those they trust. Proverbs 27:5–6 says, *"An open rebuke is better than hidden love! Wounds from a friend are better than many kisses from an enemy"* (NLT). On the other hand, many friendships have ended because of the honest, loving criticism of a faithful friend who wanted only to help. The foolish consider every opinion to be a judgment.

Even when criticism is spoken for harm, it can be turned to good if we have the heart for it. No one likes criticism, but criticism is often the only thing that will cause us to face our foolishness. Criticism is what we experience when we will not learn by teaching. What we do not hear our friends try to tell us in kindness, we will face later through the harshness of our enemies.

Learn from Criticism and Avoid the End of a Fool

Somewhere in life I picked up the idea, "Listen when your enemies criticize you. They'll tell you the truth that your friends avoid." Too many times I have learned the fool's way. The Bible says, *"A single rebuke does more for a person of understanding than a hundred lashes on the back of a fool"* (Proverbs 17:10 NLT). Remember, a fool is a person who will not learn by instruction. After instruction, there's correction. If correction is ignored, only consequences are left. Those consequences can range from criticism to personal destruction.

One night I met with a group of leaders from a church. I did not know that the pastor was having moral problems and felt very threatened by my presence in his church. He told his elders that I was there to criticize them for not reaching out to the city. He told me that he wanted me to share with his elders about how the church could be more effective at outreach. The results were disastrous. To say they reacted unfavorably would be to put it mildly. They attacked me with venom and passed some very harsh judgments on me.

After the meeting I wept and prayed. I did not weep because they had hurt me with their words; I wept because there had been something in my behavior that made it easy for them to believe the worst about me. A person who tried to destroy me did me a great favor that night. What he meant as a weapon of destruction caused one of the most positive attitude changes in my life. God can turn any negative situation into a learning experience if we are teachable.

Of course, not every criticism is a judgment. When someone criticizes our efforts, expresses dislike for us, or points out a fault, that is not judgment. That is merely observation. They are seeing something and expressing their opinion. Their opinion may be right or wrong; they may handle it in an inappropriate manner, but we can still learn from it. If people see something in us that brings them to a judgment, we must reject the judgment but accept the criticism. We must ask ourselves, "What is it in my behavior that makes them reach this judgment about me?"

The Way of the Fool

Foolish people learn only from negative experience. If they have enough bad experiences, they may finally accept a reality that they could have seen from just believing the Bible. Most of the time fools don't learn; they just keep making the same decisions on the same principles, expecting a different outcome. They repeat the same mistakes and never learn.

When the foolish begin to suffer the consequences of their actions, they are quick to play the victim. When foolish people violate the rules of society and society reacts unfavorably, they accuse society of judging them. If they fail to learn from the consequences of criticism, they enter the more painful consequences that come from living their foolishness to its ultimate end.

An earmark of the foolish is that they do not want input from the people around them. *"A fool despises his father's instruction, but he who receives correction is prudent"* (Proverbs 15:5 NKJV). When people offer them good advice that they do not want to accept as reality, they accuse those people of judging them or of attempting to run their lives. Regardless of the preferred defense mechanism, the result is the same: they keep making the same mistakes until they suffer personal destruction.

Fools seek to defend their position on verbal technicalities. Like lawyers in a courtroom, they will refute the criticism of their accusers on the basis of moot verbal distinctions. Many people live by the philosophy, "If you can't prove it, it isn't true. To prove it, you must word it all perfectly. For your accusation to be valid, it must be worded perfectly—*and* you have to catch me."

Even if our accusers reach wrong conclusions, even if they word their criticism incorrectly, even if their judgments about why we are doing what we are doing are inaccurate, we are still fools if we fail to consider their point of view. A fool will never ask how or why others see it the way they do. The fool simply responds to the observation with defensive accusations.

Listen the First Time

Unteachable fools do not understand why people come at them with such force. To use a common phrase, they are clueless! People who love them and do not want to see them hurt usually tell them the truth in a kind way. When the information is ignored, those loving friends and family say it a little more forcibly. When it is ignored again, they desperately "go for the throat." Then their hearer rejects it because it was an attack. Such people often ask me, "Why do people say things to me so strongly?" My answer is usually the same. "If you would listen when people speak gently and acknowledge their input, they would never speak to you so forcibly."

It is usually at this point that I discover the truth: "I didn't respond because it wasn't any of their business." Now we have established that you *did* hear it when they pointed out the problem the first time. However, rather than consider their input, you played the denial game and expected them to leave you alone.

People who love you will never leave you alone. However misguided their attempts, they will just speak louder and more forcibly until you at least acknowledge the situation.

Granted, not every lesson will be taught in love. Not every teacher will be seeking our good. Make no mistake, however; every person is our teacher, and every circumstance is a classroom. Winning the argument does not mean we will win at life. Verbally defeating our accuser will not deliver us from the consequences of our actions. Instead, our defensive actions usually stir the fires of accusation.

There are many ways to respond to accusation or criticism that will produce peace and personal growth rather than pain and distress. When you realize that, though everything may not be intended for your good, you can still make it work to your good, then the misguided criticism of others causes you little pain.

Twenty-five

Relationships That Work

❧

What I say doesn't mean what it means to me. It means what it means to you!

Relationships are the joy and the pain of life. Regardless of the initial reason people seek counseling, ultimately the issue revolves around a relationship. If the issue at hand seems to be about money, anger, or fear, it is usually the way that money, anger, or fear affects our ability to have relationships that causes us to do something about it.

Relationships are the only thing of eternal value in this life. All that we will take out of this world with us will be the relationships we take into eternity. Regardless of what you have materially, you will not be happy without fulfilling relationships. Most addictive, compulsive behavior revolves around the issues of relationships—or the lack thereof.

Relationships are the foundation of all growth and meaningful personal development. The only real gauge we have for personal growth is our effectiveness at developing meaningful relationships. Since relationships are built around communication, or the giving and receiving of input, we cannot have meaningful relationships unless we accept the rights of the people with whom we share our lives. In other words, in a relationship, you give other people the privilege of speaking into your life. Since your life affects them, there are no other options.

Relationship Requirements

To have loving, reciprocal relationships—that is, to give and take—we must run certain risks. Relationships thrive on communication, and communication is based on honesty. Honesty, however, creates vulnerability. For many people, vulnerability is a liability they would rather not encounter. So instead of facing the possibilities of unhappiness through pain in a relationship, they choose to live in the certainty of pain found in the absence of meaningful relationships.

Relationships that work must be reciprocal; there is give and take. They are based on our ability to share our ideas, our strengths, and our weaknesses. Through sharing, we grow, develop, and adjust to make the relationship more positive and fulfilling. Thus, flexibility and adaptability must follow all communication.

In relationships, just as in all other social interaction, we surrender some of our rights. If we care for one another, we must accept the fact that our actions affect others. As such, we cannot ask people to be in our lives and then refuse them the right to give input into our lives. "You can be in my life, but keep your opinions to yourself" is not the stuff of real relationships.

Too often we consider the input of our friends to be judgments and so refuse to adapt and benefit. But in order to grow in a relationship and as a person, we must always consider how our behavior affects the other person. When that other person gives us input, we must consider it, utilize it, and grow thereby.

Again, flexibility and adaptability are essential to all personal growth.

Few people understand how our behavior affects the people around us. Yet it is the people around us with whom we desire to have relationships. According to Robert Dilts, in his book *Applications of Neuro-Linguistic Programming,* an important communication principle says, "The meaning of any communication is the response it elicits, regardless of the intent of the communicator."* We can never know how our behavior affects other people unless we are willing to let them speak into our lives. Finding new friends is not the way to respond to unfavorable input from current friends.

Love makes us always want to know how our behavior affects those around us. In nearly every counseling session, one of the most important discoveries is made when people become aware of how their behavior affects others. Once that is realized, the other person's feedback doesn't feel like criticism. Instead, it becomes something that helps the relationship.

For many of us, the issue of change is more than we can face. To change may require that we admit to being wrong. Very often, we value being right more than we value our relationships. Our insecurity and resulting inflexibility cause us to move from person to person, looking for the relationship that will never require growth and change.

It is not judgment when someone points out that our behavior is unscriptural or unacceptable; it is meaningful input. We are often unaware when we violate the wisdom of God's Word. If we really care about walking in truth, this type of input helps us get back on course. We need constant feedback from our social surroundings in order to continually adjust our effectiveness in relationships.

* Dilts, Robert. *Applications of Neuro-Linguistic Programming.* Cupertino, Calif.: Meta Publications, 1983, 14.

Avoid Relationship Manipulation

Sometimes we accept input only from people from whom we hope to gain something. For example, teenagers will allow their friends to have more influence in their lives than their parents. A single person will allow the person she is dating to have more influence than other friends. Some people allow certain friends to have more influence than others. Too often, that influence is received because of what we hope to gain. That is not openness; that is manipulation.

The people to whom we make ourselves vulnerable should not be those from whom we hope to receive benefit. Rather, we should be vulnerable with the people who are effective in the areas in which we need input. We should be open and honest with people who are stable and have proven that they have genuine love for us. It is common knowledge that it is easy to con someone who is trying to con. When people are taking advantage of someone for gain, they become blinded by their greed and can themselves be taken advantage of. Proverbs says it this way: *"Wrongdoers listen to wicked talk; liars pay attention to destructive words"* (Proverbs 17:4 NLT). In other words, they start listening to all the wrong people.

When we begin to play the manipulation game, we always listen to the wrong people. This is often how people begin the destructive cycle of "repetitive pain," in which a person seems to encounter the same hurts in every new relationship. We violate sound principles for building relationships, and then we eat the fruit of our ways when it all goes wrong. Growing feelings of shame and desperation begin to control our lives. We refuse to hear anything that doesn't encourage us in our desperate pursuit of happiness. We close our ears to sound advice and listen only to those from whom we hope to benefit. Each relationship ends in failure, and we become emptier and more desperate; however, we refuse to abandon our destructive ways. The moral compromise

143

to get what we want becomes greater and greater. With each decision, the possibility for repetitive pain grows.

At this point in time, reasonable people attempt to provide reasonable input. The desperate person, however, does not see the input as reasonable. Instead, the desperate one sees it as limiting, controlling, and judgmental. The person always thinks his path of compromise will get him what he wants. It doesn't. Proverbs 14:12 says, *"There is a path before each person that seems right, but it ends in death"* (NLT). It is at this point that all input that does not reinforce the self-delusion is rejected as judgment.

Not everything that causes us pain is judgment, nor is it wrong. The pain comes when we judge the motive. To a guilty conscience, everything is threatening. If our hearts condemn us, anything challenging will condemn us. We will think it is the person, but it is our conscience.

So don't reject those who have been faithful just because you don't like their input. When you find yourself being defensive or reactionary, ask yourself why you are so resistant. Sometimes it is good to listen to people with whom you know you disagree, just to get another perspective. The wise learn by instruction; the slow learn by correction; the foolish learn by consequences; and the selfish never learn. Listen, learn, grow…and stop the pain.

Twenty-six

Excuse Me while I
Eat My Words

⦿

The bitterness in my life today is the words I spoke yesterday.

In our response to what we feel is judgment, it is essential that we understand the role we play in provoking others to judge us. Although it is never right for anyone to judge, it is still going to happen. It is futile for us to cry out, "Unfair! Unfair!" Such pleading will not help us in the face of our accusers. In fact, it may even provoke them to a stronger attack.

If we have sown the seeds of judgment and criticism, we can be sure that we will reap the same. *"Judge not, that ye be not judged"* (Matthew 7:1) complies with the law of sowing and reaping. People will always do to us what we have done to them—and more besides. However, there is much we can do to avoid judgment.

Proverbs 18:6 says, *"A fool's lips bring him strife, and his mouth invites a beating"* (NIV). The mouth is a small hole in the front of the face with which we create a world of problems. The way we communicate will do more to incite judgment and invite pain than anything else! Even when people's actions are unacceptable, our communication can make the consequences either better or worse.

As Proverbs says, foolish lips invite punishment. Getting control of our words is one of the key ways to change our world. Proverbs also says, *"A [self-confident] fool has no delight in understanding but only in revealing his personal opinions and himself"* (Proverbs 18:2 AMP). The desire to air our opinions may be the source of many of our tribulations. *"A fool vents all his feelings, but a wise man holds them back"* (Proverbs 29:11 NKJV). These Scriptures offer us communication insights that can help us avoid pain.

The Effects of Unintentional Words

When I first came to the Lord, my language was very rough. I don't mean I used profanity; I just spoke very harshly to people. It was the way of the street. As a result, people began to judge me as a condemning, unforgiving person. At the time I could not understand where they were coming up with these opinions; nothing was further from the truth. I was actually very caring and merciful.

No one would tell me why or where these opinions were coming from. Anyone could have said, "When you say this to me, this is how it makes me feel. Is this what you intended?" But nobody did! Instead, people simply formed their judgments and talked about me as if their judgments were correct. If only someone had followed the rules of communication.

One night, a couple was visiting my home. We were playing a game, and my partner made a very poor move. I made a threatening statement, one that I did not even mean. It was a colloquialism from the street. But I wasn't on the street; I wasn't talking to someone who understood my terminology. I was talking to someone who took my threat very seriously.

Like others whom I had offended by my rough exterior, he did not say a word to me, but I saw the look in his eyes when I said it. I knew this guy was shaken. I apologized to him, but the damage was done. There was nothing I could do at that point to take my words back or reverse the damage. I had to accept responsibility for the effect my words had on this person.

When judged or scrutinized, we often fail to accept the responsibility for how our words evoke the opinions and judgments of others. We think, *They should have known that I didn't mean that.* We are actually asking them to judge us with that thought; we just want the judgment to come out in our favor. However, we cannot expect people to read our minds. In Matthew 12:37 Jesus said, *"For by your words you will be justified, and by your words you will be condemned"* (NKJV). As someone wisely said, make your words sweet and soft. You may have to eat them.

Know What You Say—and Mean It When You Say It

Many times all we can know about someone is what we see or what we hear. Anything beyond that is judgment. When people have a low opinion of us based on our words, they are not in judgment; they are using the only information they have to form their opinion. As I said in chapter 2, words are seeds that grow in the garden of our lives. If we don't like what's growing in our garden, then we must plant different seeds.

Unfortunately, we often use words as defense mechanisms. In such cases, we tend not to think about what those words mean. We just blurt them out as a way to avoid dealing with the real issues. "I don't care" is one of the deadliest euphemisms. We rarely mean it when we say it, but it usually brings painful retaliation. We all care about the consequences of our actions. But, too often, we use "I don't care" to avoid admitting the seriousness of our actions. In the absence of any other meaningful

147

communication, while discussing important life issues, "I don't care" can be a very frightening statement. If we convince the person with whom we are communicating that we do not care, we have no right to complain when he or she treats us as if we mean it.

We should never use sarcasm and flippant answers when in the midst of meaningful communication. If we don't know the answer, we should say, "I don't know." If we don't want to talk about something, we should say, "I don't want to talk about it." If we are threatened by the way someone interrogates us, we should say, "This conversation is making me feel threatened." We should learn to say what we really mean and mean what we say. Our inappropriate responses send people wrong messages. When they respond accordingly, though, we are offended by the way they respond.

James gave a special warning to leaders.

> *My brethren, let not many of you become teachers, knowing that we shall receive a stricter judgment. For we all stumble in many things. If anyone does not stumble in word, he is a perfect man, able also to bridle the whole body.* (James 3:1–2 NKJV)

Anyone who seeks to influence, instruct, or lead another person must live by a higher standard of responsibility, especially in the area of communication.

It is not God who will judge leaders more strictly. It is people! More specifically, it is the people whom we seek to lead. The area in which they will judge us most strictly is our communication. Do we offend in the way we communicate? Is our communication clear and understandable? Are we accepting the responsibility to be a good communicator, or are we asking those around us to figure out what we really mean? When we leave it for people to figure out what we really mean, we are forcing them into the place of judgment. And we had better like the way their judgment comes out, because we will have to live with it!

> *A man's [moral] self shall be filled with the fruit of his mouth; and with the consequence of his words he must be satisfied [whether good or evil]. Death and life are in the power of the tongue, and they who indulge in it shall eat the fruit of it [for death or life].* (Proverbs 18:20–21 AMP)

When we don't like the way people are judging us, we must accept personal responsibility. Rather than lashing out and attacking, we must ask, "What am I doing or saying that provokes that kind of response?" Once we identify our role in instigating others' opinions, we have found something within our reach to solve the problem.

Twenty-seven

Confession: The Pathway to Peace

+96+

Confession frees a guilty heart.

*I*n our search for freedom from judgment, we tend to overlook one very basic principle: Confession alleviates the fear
of judgment. When a person commits a crime, he is placed
on trial, and all the evidence is brought in to convict him. Life is
much the same way. When we offend, people bring the evidence
to prove our guilt.

The way to avoid the pain and shame of a trial is to confess.
Admit it! After confession, all that's left is sentencing. Sentencing
is always more lenient for the person who confesses than for the
one who is proven guilty. Again, this is mirrored in everyday
relationships. People stop trying to convict us when we confess.
When we have told the truth, all that is left is the penalty.

Afraid to Confess

In our desperate attempt to escape pain and find pleasure, we
commit offenses. We violate others in the hope of finding some

kind of gratification. When our wrongdoing becomes apparent, people seek vindication through "conviction." We now face the shame and pain of our attitudes being exposed as well as the consequences of our actions. The more we attempt to cover our sin, the more vehemently people seek to expose us. This produces more fear and denial on our part and more ferocity on theirs.

The only hope of finding mercy is honesty. *"He who conceals his sins does not prosper, but whoever confesses and renounces them finds mercy"* (Proverbs 28:13 NIV). When we find ourselves in fault, the shortest route to peace of heart and possible forgiveness from the offended is in confession. Confession not only appeases the offended, but it also frees the guilty heart.

When people accuse us or seek to convict us, we become paralyzed. We are afraid to confess for fear of harm. Their desire for vindication forces us to protect ourselves, and our fear of confession provokes them. True, facing wrath can be short, immediate, external pain. As unappealing as that is, denial produces a lifetime of internal pain.

Confession is the only thing that frees us from the expectation of judgment. When we say why we did something, there is nothing left to judge. However, people will not confess unless they feel safe. Without a safe place to confess, they will cover over their offenses. Churches especially need to make it safe for people to confess. What constitutes a safe place? It is safe to confess when the goal of the person or church is to restore and heal. If the goal is to punish, it is never safe.

It is the fear of judgment that compels us to withhold confession. Sadly, the church has become a place where it is not safe to be honest. As a matter of fact, church, more than any other place, is where we lie about our faults and failures! Church, as a whole, has become a merciless environment that breeds deceit and hypocrisy, rather than being a safe place to be honest and grow. It actually can become a place that encourages us to wear a mask and hide our problems.

The Best Way to Process Faults

Even though we have the freedom to confess, we bind ourselves to our sin and shame. James addressed the need to process our emotions and faults: *"Is any among you afflicted? let him pray. Is any merry? let him sing psalms. Is any sick among you? let him call for the elders of the church; and let them pray over him"* (James 5:13). This is what I call "processing." We all need to process our stuff. This verse shows the biblical option that leads to life and peace. If we are afflicted, we can hold it in, think about it, and get mad and depressed, or we can process it through prayer.

If we're merry, there's a way to process it. We can have a party and get drunk and brag, or sing psalms to God, thereby processing our joy. If we're sick, we can lie in bed, complain, and seek sympathy, or we can take the biblical option and have the elders of the church pray for us. There is always a biblical way to process our issues that will lead us to life and peace.

Unfortunately, we are so out of touch with ourselves and with God that we don't really know how to process these things. Sometimes people make praise and worship a formal event rather than an expressing or processing. Praise and worship is the time to process the emotions that we feel toward God. There is a biblical way to express that. The Bible lists dozens of ways to express and process our joy, love, and thanksgiving: lifting hands, singing, dancing, bowing, and shouting, to name a few. Yet religion has stolen this freedom of expression from the church. Church has become a place where we cannot confess our faults or express our joys. That really doesn't leave much else other than rules and game playing.

James went on to tell us how to process our faults. Verse 16 says, *"Confess your faults one to another, and pray for another, that ye may be healed."* The word *fault* could be translated as "sin or offense." This is not a formal confession to a priest or a counselor. This is more than just confessing to the Lord Jesus in prayer. It is honest sharing with our friends and peers.

On the other hand, we can choose to handle our faults in an unscriptural manner: justify them, cover them up, or blame someone else for them. Any of these options may momentarily deliver us from scrutiny, but none of them will bring peace of mind. We need to know we are loved *with* our faults. We need to take off our masks and let others see us as real people who are hurting over our own offenses. We need the support of people who will help us walk through our life issues.

Live in Grace

Because we think that Christianity revolves around being "right," it has become an arena in which people seek to prove us wrong. Preachers think that their job is to get people right. However, that requires the assumption that those people are wrong. Actually, they are righteous. Jesus gave all of us the gift of righteousness; He made us as right as we can get. It is our job to help people become whole through the love of God. Paul said, *"If I must boast, I would rather boast about the things that show how weak I am"* (2 Corinthians 11:30 NLT). This is a foreign concept in Christianity today. But Paul didn't stop there. You see, he didn't demean himself as a form of false humility; rather, he had found the secret of living in God's grace/ability.

As Paul complained about his circumstances and his inability to do anything about them, God reminded Paul of the power that could work through him.

And He said to me, "My grace is sufficient for you, for My strength is made perfect in weakness." Therefore most gladly I will rather boast in my infirmities, that the power of Christ may rest upon me. Therefore I take pleasure in infirmities, in reproaches, in needs, in persecutions, in distresses, for Christ's sake. For when I am weak, then I am strong. (2 Corinthians 12:9–10 NKJV)

When God said, *"My grace is sufficient,"* He was not saying "no" to Paul's request for help. He was saying, "The circumstances don't have to change. The power to live above the control of life's circumstances and people's judgments is found in My grace/ability that works from your heart. You don't have to ask for it. It is already yours."

We have created an environment that goes to one of two extremes. Either we think weakness is humility and we are supposed to be weak all the time, or we think weakness is a failure of faith and we should never admit to it. Acknowledging our weakness and trusting God, however, should always bring us to the place of power and ability—which is God's grace to overcome.

Christianity doesn't revolve around us being right or able. It revolves around *Jesus* being right and able. But that fact becomes relevant only when we recognize that we are in Him and we partake of His strength. Being able to depend on people actually helps us depend on the Lord. Being open with people leads us to openness with God. Confessing our faults is a part of the healing process. It leads us to transparency and open communication. It helps us discover and release the places where we are stuck.

Confession Shows Up in Strange Ways

My experience tells me that people have an inherent need to confess. I've learned to listen to people when they talk. If something is bothering them, they will find an indirect way to confess it. They may not tell the exact truth, but they will tell as much as they can and still avoid judgment.

For instance, in my first church, there was a sweet woman who would talk to me from time to time. Often she would remark, "Maybe the reason my husband doesn't get saved is my fault." I would comfort her and tell her not to blame herself.

She made that remark several times. One day when I started to comfort her, the Spirit of God stopped me and showed me that I wasn't really listening to her. She was trying to tell me something. So I didn't comfort her. Instead, I began to ask what it was she was doing that had a negative effect on her husband. To my surprise, I discovered that she *was* a major influence over her husband not getting saved. The way she related to her family was very different from the way she related to those of us at church. She didn't really want to deal with the issue, but she had the need to confess.

People often create imaginary scenarios and personalities as a way of confessing. Sometimes a multiple personality disorder emerges from the need to have someone who can be the guilty party. One man told me a story about one of his family members murdering someone. The truth was, he was the one who had done it. Telling the story was simply as close to confession as he could get. However, this type of "confession" brings no relief.

Naturally, it is not wise to confess every sin to every person. But it is wise to confess those faults that cause us to offend others. Those places where we are stuck and those issues we just can't resolve in our hearts with the Lord usually have to be confessed. Unfortunately, most environments are not safe. That is why most people usually visit a priest, counselor, or pastor in his or her offices. In our church, people confess and resolve very personal issues in our Impact Groups. These small groups make it safe for people to be honest.

Confession is the only thing that frees you from the expectation of judgment. When you say what you did, you are on the way to discovering for yourself why you did it. When you say why, there is nothing left to judge. When you know you have been transparent with your faults, it doesn't matter who knows. When the heart is at peace, you can endure the opinions of others. When the heart is not at peace, every word, every look, every action feels like a judgment. And a condemned heart knows no peace.

Make it a practice to be transparent. Confess your fault, even though you know it will be unpleasant. The freedom of confessing will allow you the freedom of heart to access God's grace/ability to face any situation and emerge victorious.

Twenty-eight

Suicidal Self-Judgment

✦❧❦✦

Once we have judged ourselves, our guilty hearts create a penalty.

Of all the destructive factors related to judgment, sickness is probably the most devastating. We all know that emotional health can deteriorate through the guilt of judgment. Such guilt is based in fear and causes depression and anxiety, besides being related to every negative emotion. Unfortunately, we fail to recognize that our acceptance of judgment ravages our physical health as well. In fact, the Bible says it is a cause for sickness and death.

In his first letter to the Corinthian believers, Paul shared how Communion, or the Lord's Supper, can be a life-giving experience. Jesus had said, *"This cup is the new covenant in My blood. This do, as often as you drink it, in remembrance of Me"* (1 Corinthians 11:25 NKJV). In verse 26 Paul said that, in so doing, we *"proclaim the Lord's death till He comes"* (NKJV). Then, in verse 27, he warned us not to *"eat this bread, and drink this cup of the Lord, unworthily."* For many, the most difficult part of this passage is in attempting to understand what it means to partake unworthily!

In verse 28, we read, *"But let a man examine himself, and so let him eat of that bread, and drink of that cup."* The word *examine* means "to inspect for approval." This is not an internal audit for fault. The goal is not to look inward and determine why we are disapproved; rather, the goal is to look inward and remind ourselves of the cross of Christ, what His blood purchased for us, and why His sacrifice makes us approved.

Religion, school, and life in general have taught us to look into our own hearts and ask the question, "What's wrong with me?" We look into our hearts and say, "I have to find what is wrong so I can fix the problem." This is just the opposite of Paul's teaching. If we want to solve the problem, we have to find what's *right* with us. So Paul said, "Examine yourself for approval. Look in your heart, and try to find what brings you approval."

Our Approval Comes from Jesus

Well, what is it that brings us approval? The finished work of Jesus is the only thing that qualifies us before God. We must look to what He accomplished through His death, burial, and resurrection. He became our sin, so we don't have to live under that weight. He took the punishment for our sins, so we don't have to be afraid of punishment. He went to hell in our place, so we don't have to go to hell. He conquered our sins, so we don't have to fight that battle. He obtained righteousness and gave it to us as a free gift, so we don't have to earn it. He also qualified us for all the promises of God. In short, He is our righteousness. He is our qualification. We are approved in Him. As Colossians 2:10 says, in Him we are made complete.

Unfortunately, legalism has made us look to our works as the basis for our approval before God. However, dead works cannot cleanse our conscience. No matter what we have done right, the things we have done wrong loom over our heads like a guillotine waiting to fall in judgment. Go back to Paul's instruction—he reminded us that Communion was to be done in remembrance of Jesus and His finished work. This is not about us. It is about us in Him.

1 Corinthians 11:29 says, *"For he who eats and drinks in an unworthy manner eats and drinks judgment to himself, not discerning the Lord's body"* (NKJV). Remember, we do it unworthily when we fail to find ourselves approved in Christ. The word *judgment* here is the same as the word *condemnation*. Condemnation is a sense of guilt wherein one expects punishment. It is the result of judgment—whether self-judgment or the judgment others place on us. Regardless of the source, if we accept anyone's judgment but God's, we will find ourselves to be unworthy. Then we expect punishment.

The problem is a failure to "discern the Lord's body." In every aspect of life, we should look to Jesus and what He accomplished in His own body for us. Verse 30 says this. *"For this cause many are weak and sickly among you, and many sleep* [or many are dead].*"* The fact that we do not examine ourselves and find approval, in light of what Jesus has done on the cross, is the reason that we have sickness and death, the Bible says.

We Bring It on Ourselves

Paul continued in verse 31, *"For if we would judge ourselves, we would not be judged"* (NKJV). The Greek word used here for *judge* is a word that means "to examine, to find approval." If we would find ourselves approved, we would not experience condemnation or self-judgment. Jesus said,

> *Most assuredly, I say to you, he who hears My word and believes in Him who sent Me has everlasting life, and*

> *shall not come into judgment, but has passed from death*
> *into life.* (John 5:24 NKJV)

The problem is not that God is judging us. Rather, the judgment we experience is from our own hearts. It is called condemnation.

Hebrews 10:26–27 says,

> *For if we sin wilfully after that we have received the*
> *knowledge of the truth, there remaineth no more sacrifice*
> *for sins, but a certain fearful looking for of judgment and*
> *fiery indignation, which shall devour the adversaries.*

This passage does not say that God sends these things. It says that when we continue to willfully sin, judgment is what we ultimately experience. Because of our guilty conscience, we begin looking for things to go wrong. We start expecting judgment. We struggle with guilt. We expect punishment!

Self-judgment is a self-fulfilling prophecy. We judge that we are worthy of sickness. But when we get sick, we say, "God is punishing us." That is not true; God hasn't done anything. *We* did! Our hearts believed a lie, and we experienced the fruit of those beliefs. As Proverbs says, *"A man's own folly ruins his life, yet his heart rages against the LORD"* (Proverbs 19:3 NIV).

First Corinthians 11:32 goes on to say, *"But when we are judged, we are chastened of the Lord."* What does it mean to be chastened? The word *chasten* in the Greek language does not mean to beat, whip, punish, or execute; it means "to train a child." (See *Strong's Concordance,* #G3811.) To train a child is to draw and compel someone to walk in the right way. It is done tenderly, with great love and affection. It is not done by inflicting pain. God chastens us as the child in whom He delights.

Such training is the work of the Holy Spirit. The Bible says that the Holy Spirit will convict us in the sense of pointing us to our sin. Even when we fail to examine ourselves and find ourselves approved, the Holy Spirit will attempt to draw us into the way that will deliver us from the power and consequences of sin.

Take the case of Ananias and Sapphira. They were brand-new converts. They had not yet learned about freedom from the law and deliverance from the wrath of God. When confronted with lying to the Holy Spirit, their hearts were overwhelmed with fear and condemnation. God got blamed for killing them, but He did not strike them down. Acts 5 says that both Ananias and Sapphira *"gave up the ghost"* (verses 5, 10). God didn't kill them. The devil didn't kill them. The Greek language is very explicit about this. They were not acted upon by any outside force; something happened within them. It came from their own hearts. They believed something that was not true, and they died because of what they believed.

Your Mind Will Help You Out

In a book called *Healing Back Pain,* Dr. John Sarno, M.D., says there are thousands of people whom he has treated and made totally free of back pain without any further medical treatment than a three-hour lecture. That's all. His results are phenomenal! When we have emotional pain or other issues with which we do not know how to deal, the mind creates sickness or pain somewhere in our bodies. Having this pain gives us something legitimate to focus on so we can avoid dealing with something that we consider to be more painful. What kinds of issues are we afraid to confront that make sickness and pain more appealing? Guilt, fear, shame, feelings of unworthiness, or feelings of not being loved are at the top of the list.

Other research indicates that the mind always seeks equilibrium. It seeks to bring about or prove to be true the view that we currently hold. For example, guilt calls for punishment. When we feel guilt or shame, we have a need to be punished—so every cell in our bodies works to bring about our beliefs. If we believe we are unworthy to succeed, yet start succeeding, then our emotions, or even our physical bodies, will work to halt our success. If we believe we have done something that deserves physical punishment, we will have pain and sickness.

There are dozens of ways to influence our hearts. The most important influence is the belief that we are new creations in Jesus. We are righteous, delivered from the curse of the law, and qualified for every promise of God. This should be our general life-view. It should be the only way we think of ourselves. If it isn't, we must do whatever it takes to write this truth on our hearts!

So the next time you find yourself getting in mental torment, sickness, or pain, just sit down, relax, and open your heart to God. Then begin to acknowledge some truth. Look into your heart and say, "I don't need this pain. Regardless of what I may have done, I don't deserve this pain. Jesus took the curse of the law for me. I deserve only what Jesus died to give me."

Then acknowledge, "This pain, this sickness, this torment is not helping. It's not benefiting me. It's not bringing about any godly purpose in my life. I choose to let it go." In your heart, simply say, "I am letting this go; I am releasing this right now. Jesus, set me free from this. I don't have to have it. I'm releasing it now." Usually within minutes, you'll find that the emotion or physical pain begins to fade away.

I have shared these simple principles with people all over the world and have seen myriads set free from chronic pain and sickness. If you have negative beliefs written on your heart that have become a part of your self-perception, you may need a counselor who is trained to help you deal with heart beliefs. It may be necessary to identify the destructive judgments that have impacted you and write something new on your heart.

If you believe that the pain in your life is punishment from God, there is no relief for you. You will spend your life paying penance for your wrong. You will never be completely free from the power of sin. You will never move forward into a productive, peaceful life of walking with God and growing in character. I'm asking you to stop the pain. Stop blaming God.

By releasing yourself from judgment, you will have the opportunity to break the life cycle of chronic sickness and pain. You may never have to repeat a failed business deal or a failed relationship. You will free yourself to experience God's grace, which will make you able to live above the control of life's judgments and punishments.

Twenty-nine

Finding the Real You

❧

Find the real you, and you'll find your destiny.

W e have lived under the judgments of others and self for so long that we really believe that is who we are. We have surrendered our new identity in Christ. We have given up the realities of God for our distorted self-view. We have lost sight of the fact that we actually are new creations in Christ. Instead of seeing our limitless possibilities in Him, we live in the limited realm of our fear and judgment. We have lost our destiny by accepting our judgments as reality—and the loss of destiny results in a lifetime of disappointment and frustration.

Like kings who have amnesia, we walk around as paupers, not knowing that we are royalty. You see, every individual lives out of his or her self-perception. We can change circumstances, physical surroundings, and everything else, but if our self-perception does not change, we will continue to be governed by the same factors. We can give our sin new excuses; we can even give it a new social status—but it is still sin. We can lose weight or get cosmetic surgery; we can change our material or physical world as often as we like, but we will still feel the same way on the inside.

It Is Not about the External

Because we have been trained to be externalists, we try to feel better about ourselves by adjusting everything on the outside. In his first letter to the church, the apostle Peter wrote specific instruction to the women: *"Do not let your adornment be merely outward; arranging the hair, wearing gold, or putting on fine apparel; rather let it be the hidden person of the heart"* (1 Peter 3:3–4 NKJV). This is a life-principle that applies to everyone.

Of course, we all should take some pride in our appearance. Taking pride in our appearance is often a reflection of self-worth. Nevertheless, as the *New Living Translation* of verse 4 says, *"You should be known for the beauty that comes from within."* We can ask ourselves, "Do I want people to know me for who I am or how I look? Do I want to have relationships that go deeper than the external? Or do I want to keep all relationships shallow?" It is this very issue that promotes many relationship problems. As Peter implied, beauty fades. When our beauty fades or when a better beauty comes into our world, we have nothing else to offer the person who knows us only externally.

I am not saying we should reject external beauty; rather, we should simply keep it in its place. We should, at the very least, put as much effort into internal beauty as we do in the external. Keep in mind that developing inner beauty is not a process of acquiring something that we do not have. It is simply becoming aware of and yielding to that which is in us by Christ Jesus. When Jesus Christ came into our hearts, He brought righteousness and power. He brought a quality of life that can be found only in Him. We are not trying to get Him to give it to us. Our part is to look into our hearts and discover this new "me" on the inside.

Even when we attempt to develop character, we still tend to make it an external thing. We endeavor to create a performance-based identity. We still attempt to know who we are apart from trusting God. When satan came to tempt Jesus, he tried to deceive Him into proving His identity by His performance. *"Now when the tempter came to Him, he said, 'If You are the Son of God, command that these stones become bread'"* (Matthew 4:3 NKJV). *The Living Bible* says, *"It will prove you are the Son of God."*

Jesus refused to use His works to prove His identity. Instead, He said, *"It is written"* (verse 4). What God had spoken was sufficient for Him. That would be His source of identity.

This new nature should produce good works—we should endeavor to live a life of good works. But our trust, our confidence, and our sense of identity can never come from those works. The moment that happens, we have shifted our trust and our focus from Jesus to ourselves. At that moment, what were once good works now become dead works.

If we judge our identity by our performance, we will falter when our works do not prove who we are. If our works prove our identity, we will exalt our righteousness above the righteousness of Christ. Our righteousness is not greater than His. So we must look to the Word of God and the Spirit of God in our hearts to establish our identity. It takes both. We find the truth in the Word, but we experience the reality of that Word through a heartfelt relationship with Jesus.

Because we have failed to renew our minds, we still see ourselves, to some degree, the way we were before we got saved. Through our self-judgment, we determine that, because we have unacceptable traits on the outside, our inside must be corrupt. Most people don't want to look into their hearts because they are afraid of what they will see. They are convinced that they will see something so hideous that they will be unable to bear it.

There is a "hidden man" of the heart, a new person or nature that we are not really in touch with. Our self-judgments have kept him hidden beyond our perception. When the apostle

Paul talked about putting an end to unacceptable behavior, he pointed to the fact that we have *already* been made new. But we must change the way we think in order to "put on" the new person. The *New Living Translation* says, *"There must be a spiritual renewal of your thoughts and attitudes"* (Ephesians 4:23). We don't need to *become* something new if we are in Christ. We do, however, need to get our thinking straight. Like the earlier example of a king with amnesia, we don't need to *become* kings; we simply need to remember that we *are* kings. *"You must display a new nature because you are a new person, created in God's likeness—righteous, holy, and true"* (verse 24 NLT).

There is a new you on the inside. You think you are not new because you still have the behavior of the old you. You never accepted God's judgment on the old you: "My old man is crucified with Christ." The old sin nature was judged, found guilty, crucified, died, and was buried in Christ. You are now a new creation. You are created in the likeness and righteousness of God. The old is gone; the new has come.

Apart from our becoming new creations, salvation is worthless in this life. That sounds like a hard statement, but we did not get saved to squander our lives in sin and failure as we await heaven. No, we must use the principles of prayer, study of the Word, and biblical meditation and confession to persuade our hearts of this reality here on earth. We must spend time communing with Jesus in our hearts to create an ever-present awareness of His presence in our lives here.

The apostle Peter said that it would be through this knowledge that we would experience everything that pertains to life and godliness. *"His divine power has given to us all things that pertain to life and godliness, through the knowledge of Him who called us by glory and virtue"* (2 Peter 1:3 NKJV). If this is not real to us, we will not experience it in this life.

It Is Time to Make a Change

Just as the apostle Paul discovered, we must release ourselves and everyone around us from the shackles of our judgment. The external can no longer dictate our sense of reality, so we must stop evaluating others by what the world thinks of them.

> *Once I mistakenly thought of Christ that way, as though he were merely a human being. How differently I think about him now! What this means is that those who become Christians become new persons. They are not the same anymore, for the old life is gone. A new life has begun!* (2 Corinthians 5:16–17 NLT)

Discover the hidden man of the heart, and experience the power of transformation. Listen to your heart. Anything you find in your heart that you do not like is not the real you. It is merely a facade. It is a false belief that was put on you through your self-judgment. If you look long enough, you will find the real you—created in the likeness and image of God.

When you seek this reality with all your heart, you will find it. When you live out of your new identity, you have found the real you—and the pathway to your destiny.

Thirty

Gaining a New Perspective

🙵

How I see it is not how it is, but how I will experience it.

"The LORD is my shepherd....He restores my soul" (Psalm 23:1, 3 NIV). God's goal is to restore our souls—that is, our emotions, our minds, and our thoughts. He wants to lead us to a place of still waters and green pastures. He wants us to find peaceful emotions. In Matthew 11:29, Jesus said that if we would follow Him, we would find rest for our souls.

Sin destroys the soul. Ezekiel 18:20 says, *"The soul that sinneth, it shall die."* The moment we participate in sin of any kind, it begins to influence our souls, our emotions, and our thoughts. Our way of thinking changes; our emotions are altered. Paul said in Ephesians 4:18 that sin "darkens" our understanding. In other words, the way we see and comprehend things begins to change.

We are like Adam. God said Adam would die if he ate of the fruit. Adam must have wondered why he didn't fall over dead after eating it. Perhaps he thought his sin had no real consequence.

Yet he changed emotionally. However subtle it was at first, the change in his emotions caused him to be afraid of and hide from God. He saw God differently. He saw his world differently.

The apostle John said, *"Beloved, I pray that you may prosper in all things and be in health, just as your soul prospers"* (3 John 2 NKJV). In this brief Scripture, we gain an incredible insight. We can prosper and be in good health *only* if we are prospering in the realm of the soul, the mind, and the emotions. When sin affects our souls, we begin to see and experience life differently. We find ourselves doing things we never believed we would do. Life becomes a downhill spiral—until we allow God to restore our souls.

Sin Changes Our View

The emptiness of sin leaves us hungering for real life and happiness. Yet the darkening of our understanding leads us to believe that happiness is found in more sin. Some people never break out of this cycle. Once we feed the hunger of self-indulgence, we find it to be a bottomless pit that is never satisfied. It is a dark prison from which there is no escape. When speaking of the cravings that come from greed, Proverbs 30:15 says, *"The leech has two daughters; Give and Give!"* (NKJV). Likewise, once the spiral of self-centeredness begins, there is no satisfying it.

Isaiah prophesied of Jesus, *"You will open the eyes of the blind, and release those who sit in prison darkness and despair"* (Isaiah 42:7 TLB). The darkness that holds people is the unquenchable longing of self-centeredness; it is the despair and disappointment that come from carnal attempts at gratification; it is the deceitfulness of sin.

Remember, self-centeredness judges everything and everyone in its environment in light of self. It considers only one perspective: How does this affect me? People who succumb to the cunning of self-centeredness enter a state of darkness and pain that cannot be healed. The prison in which they sit is one created from the distorted perceptions of self-centered judgment. They really believe that people are doing things because of them, that people really are trying to hurt them. All of life becomes a sore, an open wound that will not heal because it is continually reopened at every turn of events.

In Luke 4:18–19 Jesus said,

> *The Spirit of the LORD is upon Me, because He has anointed Me to preach the gospel to the poor; He has sent Me to heal the brokenhearted, to proclaim liberty to the captives and recovery of sight to the blind, to set at liberty those who are oppressed; to proclaim the acceptable year of the LORD.* (NKJV)

In order for God to set you free from your bondage and restore your soul, He must first recover your sight.

Though Jesus obviously opened physically blind eyes, we know that physical healing alone will not bring people out of the darkness of oppression. The eyes of the heart must be opened as well if they are to see their way clearly enough to come out of their prison.

Open Your Eyes to God's Perspective

In Mark 6, Jesus fed the five thousand with just five loaves and two fish. Since Jesus was a man *"in all points tempted as we are, yet without sin"* (Hebrews 4:15 NKJV), He must have faced an incredible internal struggle before working this miracle. The situation had to have looked overwhelming. Just like all overwhelming situations, it must have looked as if there was no way of escape, no way to find a happy end.

In Mark 6:41 we read,

> *And when He had taken the five loaves and the two fish, He looked up to heaven, blessed and broke the loaves, and*

171

> *gave them to His disciples to set before them; and the two*
> *fish He divided among them all.* (NKJV)

The phrase *"looked up to heaven"* is the same Greek phrase used in Luke 4:18 that is translated as "recover sight."

When Jesus was overwhelmed by the need to feed so many with such limited resources, He looked into heaven and "recovered sight." Before He could work a miracle, He had to see things from God's perspective. Had He continued to view His situation from His own limited perspective as a man, He would have been taken captive by the problem. No miracle would have happened.

At this point, Jesus could have entered into judgment. "Why is this happening to Me? Why are all these people putting all this pressure on Me? Why does everyone expect so much of Me? Why is God letting this happen?" Had He turned to judgment, He would have been taken captive by and limited to His own judgment. Instead, He released Himself from the limitation of judgment and entered the limitless realm of God's perspective.

People do not live in poverty, sickness, and sorrow because God has left them. Neither do they need more of God. You see, when we were born again, all that God is came into us by His Spirit. We simply need to be freed from the self-imposed restrictions of our judgment. We need to see our potential from God's perspective. We need to recover sight.

We who believe in the promises of God may call out to Him to break demon powers, but nothing happens because it is not the devil who is restricting us. We may pray for the circumstance to change; we may pray for the depression or fear to leave—but these things can't change or leave as long as we cling to our point of view and our judgments. Captivity is a stronghold of beliefs, not of demonic powers. Deliverance can come only when we have "recovered sight."

Paul said it like this:

> *For the weapons of our warfare are not carnal, but mighty through God to the pulling down of strong holds; casting down imaginations, and every high thing that exalteth itself against the knowledge of God, and bringing into captivity every thought to the obedience of Christ.*
>
> (2 Corinthians 10:4–5)

Strongholds are the vain imaginations and beliefs that conflict with the knowledge we have about God.

The ultimate bondage is living for self. As long as we see the world from our judgment, we will remain captive to everything that hurts us. But when we, like Jesus, turn to God to recover our sight, we will find complete victory over every circumstance. God's way is not narrow and difficult; His way is spacious and free. Jesus said it was easy and light (Matthew 11:30).

Let's surrender our view and opinion to God's, so that we might always see a way to live in victory. When we see God's view, peace replaces fear, love consumes hate, and understanding conquers confusion. When we see from God's perspective, we are able to follow Him to the place of green pastures and still waters. Then our souls are restored, and we have peace.

Thirty-one

Freedom from the Pain of the Past

❖

We will never be free to pursue our future until we are free from the pain of the past.

Trying to forget the pain of the past doesn't heal the pain. Unresolved issues can linger vaguely in the back of our minds and become a tormenting vexation, which is something that consumes. This vexation dominates our attention; it becomes the focus of our thoughts; it renders us incapable of giving our attention to the present because we are stuck in the past.

Jesus taught that there was no way to avoid offense (Matthew 18:7). There is no place of spirituality where we can avoid it. However, an offense does not need to become a vexation that torments, dominates, or influences our entire lives. Pain is unavoidable, but torment is optional. We can prevent pain from bursting into the fires of vexation by making meaningful decisions.

Whatever You Focus on Will Grow

First of all, *where* we focus our attention can intensify our experience. Often, when we become vexed, we magnify the problems, fears, temptations, or pains beyond proportion. As a result, they become the focus of our life experience. They become the matrix around which our lives and emotions are formed. In one sense, vexation is the opposite of worship. Actually, it may even be a form of worship. Psalm 34:3 says, *"Oh, magnify the LORD with me, and let us exalt His name together"* (NKJV). *To magnify* means "to make louder, larger, and mightier." We cannot actually make God any mightier than He is, but we can make our experience of Him mightier. We do that as we focus on and exalt Him. Likewise, our problems and pains seem to grow larger when we focus our attention on them. This is how vexation begins.

Anything on which we focus our attention is made larger in our experience. We can magnify a fault or annoyance in a person to the extent that we lose all respect for him or her, regardless of any other positive quality he or she has. In many cases the thing we magnify is incredibly insignificant. Yet, because of the way we allow it to affect us, it can destroy an entire friendship.

When we become vexed with something, it becomes so large in our minds that it can control our lives. Ironically, we are often drawn to those things that vex us, even if we hate them. Why? There is a scriptural principle that says we become what we behold. That is the very principle God uses to transform us. We behold an image of God, and we are transformed into His likeness. Or we hold a positive quality in our minds, and we find ourselves expressing that quality. Conversely, if we hold in our minds an image of someone we hate, we will become like that person.

I hated my father, yet as a young man, I found myself becoming more and more like him. In my counseling ministry,

I continually find people who have become the image of what they hate. You see, we don't stop doing something by thinking about it all the time. To think about anything is to magnify it in our experience.

How to Avoid Vexation

Beliefs of the heart are established by a combination of information and experience. When we go through a strong emotional event, the information we combine with that event becomes the way we interpret the event. It becomes our reality. Often when people hurt us, they speak words that we believe to be true. The abuser makes statements like, "You know you wanted this." Many children grow up to spend their entire lives believing it was their fault they were molested. That information, at the moment of strong emotion, became a heart belief.

Far too often, the information in our minds, at the time of painful emotion, is the judgment we expressed through self-talk. Since our judgment determines why people did what they did "to us," their actions become about us. When you think about it, we have a tremendous capacity to endure pain. Most events would have little effect on our lives apart from the judgments that forge deep, heartfelt beliefs. What could have been a momentary pain instead becomes suffering through judgment. Our judgment gives the action significance in our lives. It makes a statement about us and why things happen to us. That pain is then magnified through vexation until it becomes a consuming torment.

Let me reiterate that we never really remember anything the way it happened. Instead, we remember the way it made us feel. Also, some studies indicate that we never remember anything the same way. Each time we remember an experience, we remember how it made us feel the last time we thought of it. Thus, our painful experience grows with time. In other words, every time we remember, it grows in intensity and pain, and that increased intensity creates new significance. Hence, we spend our lives in vexation and torment.

Jesus warned against vexation in Luke 21:34.

> *Be careful, or your hearts will be weighed down with dissipation, drunkenness and the anxieties of life, and that day will close on you unexpectedly like a trap.* (NIV)

When our attention is consumed with pain, sin, greed, lust, or any other vexation, we become unable to walk through life aware. Trouble befalls us seemingly without warning. Although it is clear to any onlooker, we never see it coming. We are weighed down, consumed with burdens and pains. Our feeling of having no control over life grows. A victim's mentality overcomes our confidence. We lose our lives because we have lost our souls. We become like Lot, a righteous man who became vexed. *"For that righteous man dwelling among them, in seeing and hearing, vexed his righteous soul from day to day with their unlawful deeds"* (2 Peter 2:8).

Release People, and You Will Become Free

We assume that we can recover from the past simply by forgiving people who have hurt us. That is only one part of recovery. Another major part of recovery from the past comes when we release people, including ourselves, from our judgments. We really don't know why the people in our past did the hurtful things they did. We don't even know why we did many of the shameful things we did. Chances are that people did some of those hurtful things because they themselves were hurting on the inside. Their actions had very little to do with us, but we judged them as if they did. We said, "The reason they did this is they didn't love me," or "I was unlovable," or "I was a bad child." In reality, they were just doing what they were doing, and we happened to be there.

Until we release these people from our judgment, the torment of the past will not go away. Regardless of how many times we say, "I forgive you," bitterness and anger will constantly reemerge. Of course, we are not approving of what they did. We are not saying it is all right. But we are not releasing them from judgment for *them*; we are doing it for *ourselves*. Too often we forgive because we think it is an act of kindness toward the offender. In reality, it is an incredible act of kindness toward us.

Today may be the day you need to sit down alone and release someone in the past from your judgment. Some people have found it helpful to actually write these feelings out in a letter that may never be mailed. It is not for the other person; it is for you. In this letter, you should state what happened, how it made you feel, how it affected your life, and the judgments you passed about yourself and the other person. Then write out specifically how you choose to release the person from that judgment and how you choose to view this situation.

Read your letter aloud. Experience the release of judgment and the pain that it brought. Give yourself freedom from the control of that situation. Accept God's forgiveness for living in judgment. Experience God's grace to live above the problem. Then, burn the letter. As you watch it be consumed by the flames and dissipate into a cloud of smoke, see your past pain doing the same thing. Then live your life free from the pain of the past! There are dozens of ways to release yourself from past pain and judgment. It really doesn't matter which method you choose as long as you take the steps. Do what it takes to be free from your past so that you can discover the wonderful future God has for you!

Thirty-two

Living out of God's Judgment

❄❄❄

My self-perception is distorted by my self-judgments.

"*J*esus said, 'For judgment I have come into this world, so that the blind will see and those who see will become blind'*" (John 9:39 NIV). According to R. C. H. Lenski, in *The Interpretation of St. John's Gospel,* the Greek word for *judgment* in this Scripture refers to the "verdict of judgment."* This is God's verdict of the world: "If you are blind, I will give you sight. If you insist that the way you see it is reality, you will become blind."

The Message presents this so clearly.

> *Jesus then said, "I came into the world to bring everything into the clear light of day, making all the distinctions clear, so that those who have never seen will see, and those who have made a great pretense of seeing will be exposed as blind." Some Pharisees overheard him and*

---

* Lenski, R. C. H. *The Interpretation of St. John's Gospel.* Columbus, Ohio: Lutheran Book Concern, 1931.

*said, "Does that mean you're calling us blind?" Jesus said,
"If you were really blind, you would be blameless, but
since you claim to see everything so well, you're account-
able for every fault and failure."* (John 9:39–41)

By their own standards, the Pharisees judged themselves
righteous. Self-righteousness, however, does not always declare
itself as righteousness. A form of self-righteousness sometimes
will declare itself as unrighteousness. It is just as self-righteous
to declare ourselves unrighteous, when we have been declared
righteous, as it is to be unrighteous and declare ourselves as
righteous. The sin of self-righteousness is not the particular verdict that is reached; it is the fact that we choose our own standards over God's standards. There is only one righteousness
that is acceptable before God: the righteousness that He gives us
freely in Jesus. Anything else requires that we be judged by our
performance—but no one has ever been declared righteous by
his or her deeds.

We must accept God's judgment and see ourselves as He sees
us. We cannot allow ourselves to hold a view or opinion that violates God's view and opinion. If we do hold opposing views, we
are among those who insist that they see, only to find that their
opinion has blinded them to God's reality. People who cling to
their own standard of righteousness will never see and experience the incredible liberation of God's righteousness. They will
labor under a painful burden of attempting to earn righteousness.

What God Did about It

God's verdict found the entire world guilty and deserving of
death. *"Now we know that whatever the law says, it says to those
who are under the law, that every mouth may be stopped, and
all the world may become guilty before God"* (Romans 3:19 NKJV).
Because the entire world was guilty and hopeless, He sentenced

us to death in our sins. God's righteousness required that all mankind be declared guilty. His righteousness required that every person pay the penalty of eternal death for his or her sin.

However, God is a loving Father who never wants His children to experience pain or suffering. So He made a way that would ensure that every person had an equal opportunity. He sent Jesus to planet Earth as a man. Man (Adam) brought sin into the world, and a man (Jesus) had to take sin out of the world. Jesus lived a sinless life, and at the end He was nailed to a cross. While on that cross, God made Him to become the sins of the entire world (Isaiah 53:6; 2 Corinthians 5:21). He became our sin so that He could take all our punishment, thereby freeing us from the punishment of sin (Isaiah 53:4–5; Galatians 3:13).

The apostle Paul said it this way: *"I have been crucified with Christ"* (Galatians 2:20 NKJV). Jesus' death on the cross was God's judgment against our sin.

> *For we know that our old self was crucified with him so that the body of sin might be done away with, that we should no longer be slaves to sin—because anyone who has died has been freed from sin.*   (Romans 6:6–7 NIV)

Your old self, with all its sins, limitations, and the judgments that you passed against it, is dead. That is God's judgment.

However, His judgment does not stop there. If we accept His judgment of death, then we must accept His judgment of life: *"In the same way, count yourselves dead to sin but alive to God in Christ Jesus"* (verse 11 NIV). The God who said that our old self was unrighteous and worthy of death is the same God who said that in Christ we are new creations, made righteous by His blood, sanctified and holy. (See Romans 5:9; 1 Corinthians 6:11; 2 Corinthians 5:17; Colossians 1:22; Hebrews 10:14.) We stand approved before God, qualified for every promise He ever made.

(See 2 Corinthians 1:20; Ephesians 1:6; Colossians 1:12.) But all of this is based on our acceptance of the finished work of Jesus.

Believe You Are Who God Says You Are

Our primary effort for personal development must be to accept who we are in Jesus. We must establish our hearts in this new identity, or we will spend our lives in the limiting self-judgment of the past. We must never think of ourselves in any terms other than those declared by God. We must never interpret our actions in light of our judgment; we are who God says we are and who Jesus has made us to be. We have no other identity.

God will never have another judgment of us. Unlike those who reject His judgment, we will never stand under the Great White Throne judgment. When we stand before Christ, we will not undergo personal scrutiny. The only thing that will be judged is our works. We have already been judged, and we accepted the penalty of death on all that we were. (See John 5:24; 1 Corinthians 3:13–15; 2 Corinthians 5:10.) There is no other judgment from God than that which is already determined. Our unacceptable works will be burned, but we will be accepted. Because those works are burned, we will have no shame as we stand before our Lord, clothed completely in His righteousness.

Jesus said, "The glory that the Father has given Me, I give to you." (See John 17:22.) We are the glory of God in the earth. Our lives should be a reflection of His love, character, and provision. People should be able to look at us and see the greatness of God. Contrary to popular belief, perfection is not the greatest reflection of God. Jesus did not say, "They will believe you are My disciples when all your problems are solved." No, He said, *"By this all will know that you are My disciples, if you have love for one another"* (John 13:35 NKJV). God's perfection is revealed in perfect love.

The world must see people who are free from the feelings of judgment and free from passing judgment. Only when we stop judging and are able to love one another, in spite of our faults, will the world will see the glory of God in us. The glory of a father is never revealed in a rejected child.

So do not insist that you see; do not reject God's judgment for your own. When you release your judgment, your blindness will go away, and you will see yourself from God's perspective: forgiven, made righteous, and accepted.

God's judgment of us does not leave us in the grave; rather, it raises us up into newness of life! His judgment is just and good. It does not leave us in the weakness of our sin, but seats us with Him in heavenly places, empowered by His grace.

Thirty-three

Life without Limits

❧

*Our self-judgments have set the limitations and boundaries
for our lives.*

As we release ourselves and others from judgment, we enter
into a new realm of freedom and opportunity. The clearly
defined boundaries that once controlled our lives give
way to a new vision. We cross the limits that once controlled
us, hardly noticing that they ever existed. This releasing of judgments is the pathway to life without limits.

Jesus has plainly said, *"With God all things are possible"*
(Matthew 19:26). Paul boldly declared, *"I can do all things
through Christ who strengthens me"* (Philippians 4:13 NKJV).
These are not the real beliefs of most Christians. Few people
accept these concepts as a spiritual reality. We have reduced
these verses to platitudes that have no bearing on our lives. We
all believe God can do anything; we are just not so sure He can
do anything through us! Our self-judgments have exempted us
from the Word of God and from the finished work of Jesus.

Psalm 78:41 says of the children of Israel, *"Yea, they turned
back and tempted God, and limited the Holy One of Israel."*
The children of Israel had promises from God, but they made

judgments about themselves that limited God. When the twelve spies went to spy out the Promised Land, they came back with this report: *"There we saw the giants (the descendants of Anak came from the giants); and we were like grasshoppers in our own sight, and so we were in their sight"* (Numbers 13:33 NKJV).

Their enemies did not see them as grasshoppers; the children of Israel saw themselves as grasshoppers. This judgment was the beginning of forty years of wandering aimlessly in the wilderness, where time and time again they limited God. The writer of the letter to the Hebrews compared us to them: *"For indeed the gospel was preached to us as well as to them; but the word which they heard did not profit them, not being mixed with faith in those who heard it"* (Hebrews 4:2 NKJV). God's promises are of no benefit to us when we make them subservient to our self-judgments. When we exalt our imaginations above the knowledge of God, they create the strongholds that limit our dreams and successes.

In Christ, We Are Limitless

Accepting God's judgment removes us from the limitations of self-judgment. This is how we enter the limitless dimensions of His grace. Then the past no longer controls us; previous experiences no longer establish our future opportunities. We become free to be who God says we are. We can let go of the old life and all its fears and slip into the new life.

In Ecclesiastes 8:14, Solomon said,

> *There is a vanity which occurs on earth, that there are just men to whom it happens according to the work of the wicked; again, there are wicked men to whom it happens according to the work of the righteous. I said that this also is vanity.* (NKJV)

Like Solomon, many people look at the children of God and determine that there is no benefit in walking with God. After all,

Christians don't have it any better than anyone else. Again, our judgment concerning why it happens this way leads us to deception.

Fortunately, Solomon did not stop with this frustrating observation. In Ecclesiastes 9:11 he said,

> *I returned and saw under the sun that; the race is not to the swift, nor the battle to the strong, nor bread to the wise, nor riches to men of understanding, nor favor to men of skill; but time and chance happen to them all.*
> (NKJV)

Winning the battle is not always about strength. Riches are not always about understanding. The key to winning is not in possessing great strength or a mystical blessing from God. The key is in seeing and seizing the opportunities that come our way. Most people do not see. They are blinded by the walls of limitation they have built through self-judgment.

Our self-perception determines whether a situation looks like an opportunity or a threat. I personally have seen people succeed where I was afraid to venture. My lack of confidence kept me from many successes that were well within my reach. At the same time, I also have succeeded where others failed. Do you see how we all are limited by our self-perception? When we remove the false, deceptive limits of personal judgment, our self-perception becomes God's perception. We can then see ourselves in Christ, empowered by His grace, able to do all things through Him.

Your Body Will Do What You Believe

Right at this moment, every cell in your body is working to bring about your self-perception. Every cell is working to create self-imposed limits or incredible freedom. For example, if you believe that you don't deserve success, every cell in your body will work to keep you from having success. You could get sick and lose your job or have a bad attitude toward a good job, and so fulfill your deeply believed judgments.

If you believe you do not deserve love, every cell in your body will work to guide you away from loving relationships. Feelings of jealousy or uncertainty may crop up that prevent the trust necessary for developing a growing relationship. Unexplained anger may rise up and destroy the relationship. Or you could repeatedly choose a person with whom it is impossible to develop love.

All those limits and impenetrable boundaries are removed when you release yourself from your own judgments. When you accept that your old self, with all its faults and judgments, has already died, and that now you are a new person in Christ, you cross over from limitation into freedom.

Proverbs 18:9 in the *Amplified Bible* says, *"He who does not use his endeavors to heal himself is brother to him who commits suicide."* Doing nothing to establish your heart in your new identity in Jesus is equivalent to committing suicide. Every day that you stay in your old mind-set, your self-judgments steal some of the abundant life from you. Like the children of Israel, you limit God.

Every moment of your life could be fulfilling. Every love could be deep and passionate. Every friendship could be rewarding, and every job successful. You really can live the abundant life if you believe the truth about who you are in Jesus. How? Every day for the rest of your life, spend time persuading yourself of your new identity.

Thirty-four

The Self-Worth Solution

❧

I am worth what God paid for me!

The need for self-worth factors into our every strength and weakness. We make every decision in light of our sense of self-worth, which inspires us to act either in confident boldness or in timidity and fear.

Mankind's introduction into the world was with honor.

> *You have made him a little lower than the angels; You have crowned him with glory and honor, and set him over the works of Your hands. You have put all things in subjection under his feet.* (Hebrews 2:7–8 NKJV)

The phrase *"glory and honor"* can be translated as "dignity and worth." God's intention was for man to have dignity and worth!

Exactly What Happened in the Garden?

Adam did not rule the world out of carnal power, but out of a sense of dignity and worth. His feelings of worth emerged from his relationship with his Creator, Father, and God. Because of who he was in relationship to God, he experienced love and acceptance from God and felt right about himself.

When Adam became a sinner, he became fearful. Out of fear, his heart condemned him before God. As Colossians says, people's wicked actions make them feel alienated from God. *"And you, who once were alienated and enemies in your mind by wicked works, yet now He has reconciled"* (Colossians 1:21 NKJV). God has never been our enemy, yet a guilty conscience always makes us feel like He is our enemy.

Shame and guilt not only made Adam afraid of God, but they also caused him to lose his sense of identity and worth. When people feel that they are of no value to God, they have to find value through accomplishments and conquests. Thus the lust for power and control becomes a flawed replacement for the worth that comes from knowing and believing God's value.

Through the self-centeredness of the sin/fear nature, we have passed judgments about why people did things "to us." We have reached a verdict about ourselves based on our faulty judgments. And, like Adam, we also passed judgments about God. When God came to visit Adam in the Garden, Adam judged that He was there to harm him. So in this vacuum of self-worth and the fear of God, we look to others to find our value. We use the actions of others as the gauge to determine our worth.

The greater our need for self-worth, the more hypersensitive we are to the actions of others and the more we constantly evaluate ourselves to find validation and worth. We interpret every word and action in light of our existing self-need. Low self-worth thrives on judgment like a "junkie" on his drug of choice. Although it is destroying him, he doesn't know how to survive without it.

Our present sense of value is determined either by how we see ourselves in Jesus or by how we see ourselves in relation to others. Our perception is based on our judgments about why people do what they do. It is an endless ride of ups and downs based on the actions of others.

The Source of Self-Worth Is...?

God's love is the only source of abiding self-worth. His love demonstrates our value to Him. The apostle John said,

> *In this the love of God was manifested toward us, that God has sent His only begotten Son into the world, that we might live through Him. In this is love, not that we loved God, but that He loved us and sent His Son to be the propitiation for our sins.*   (1 John 4:9–10 NKJV)

God's love is not revealed only in the fact that Jesus died for us. Instead, it is specifically revealed in the fact that He became our sin, took all our punishment, obtained our righteousness, and then gave it to us as a free gift. The word *propitiation* means "appeasing of anger." Jesus was our propitiation; He fulfilled all the righteous requirements of the law. The law required that every sinner pay the full price for his or her sin. It said that no imperfection could exist with God. Jesus fulfilled the law by becoming our sin, taking all the punishment we deserved, and obtaining our righteousness. Thus God's wrath was appeased. Now God is not angry with anyone. His wrath is satisfied.

In light of this incredible act of love, we discover how despicable it is for us to reject God's free gift in favor of our own righteousness. When we look to our performance to establish our worth, we are saying, "What Jesus did is not enough!" The Great White Throne judgment will be for those who say, "I don't want the righteousness that God gives. I choose to be judged by my own works."

Jesus was God's only begotten Son. We are worth so much to God that He sent Jesus to suffer at the hands of a judgmental, religious world, become sin, take all the curse of the law, go to hell, obtain righteousness, and be raised from the dead. That price, that great love, should be the one and only source of our worth. Jesus' actions reveal our exact worth to God.

We live in a day when people look to the circumstances of life to determine God's love. If things are going well, we assume that we are doing all the right things and that God is showing His love by blessing us. If negative things are happening, we judge why they are happening: "God must not be blessing me because...." This subjective religious judgment rejects the finished work of Jesus as the absolute revelation of God's love. It chooses instead to judge God on a daily basis through the distorted view of circumstances.

When Jesus' sacrifice becomes the source of our worth, we are freed from the need to use and judge others. We also can free people from "proving" their love for us. We can release everyone in our world from our judgment and live in the great love of God.

When your emotions are generated by the finished work of Jesus, you enjoy emotional stability. Other people's actions do not affect your sense of worth. Instead of spending every moment of every day in judgment, you are free to walk in love and reach out to others. You become a giver instead of a taker. You become a servant instead of a judge. You live free from suffering.

You can't rule in life as a "King's kid" until you have a sense of dignity and worth. The self-worth issue is at the root of every decision and every action. Until the self-worth issue is settled, you will use people and events to bolster your struggling sense of worth. You will perpetuate the judgment cycle. Establishing your self-worth through the finished work of Jesus will free you to experience a level of peace and love that is beyond your wildest dreams. Take the plunge!

Thirty-five

Removing the
Splinter

⊶⊷

When I seek to fix you, I have rejected you.

There is something in our negative, fear-based thinking that has led us to believe that teaching people what is right starts by showing or telling them that they are wrong. The rationale is that if they know they are wrong, then they will want to do what is right. As a result, we Christians try to convince people that they are sinners before we tell them about God's love.

In our works-righteousness mentality (where we think we must earn righteousness), we believe that being right and knowing the truth is what qualifies us to instruct others. It seems that the entire world thrives on the need to be right. "I am right, and that qualifies me to help you!" Naturally, this creates the superiority-based separation between "clergy and laity"—the right ones and the wrong ones. Ultimately, many attempts to instruct turn into battles of "Who's right?" Being right does not qualify us to teach others. It is loving, caring, and knowing the truth that qualifies us to teach.

Your First Job: Remove the Log from Your Own Eye

Jesus gave us the prerequisite for instructing others:

And why worry about a speck in the eye of a brother when you have a board in your own? Should you say, "Friend, let me help you get that speck out of your eye," when you can't even see because of the board in your own? Hypocrite! First get rid of the board. Then you can see to help your brother. (Matthew 7:3–5 TLB)

In other words, I need to deal with me before I attempt to deal with you.

The way to truly help others is to remove the log from our own eye. We must deal with ourselves if we want to benefit someone else. We have to realize that our role is never to fix another, but to serve him. Too often we try to lead from a position of superiority. We falsely assume that if people see us as superior, they will desire to follow us and will be open to our instruction.

I once heard this said: "The person who will influence you the most is not the person you believe in; it is the person who believes in you." People trust those who believe in them. Those people are the ones with whom they feel safe enough to open their hearts and hear instruction.

We must remove from our eye the thing that blinds us to the real needs of others—and that's judgment. It is impossible to minister to them and judge them at the same time. We can't point out their faults and still make them feel safe. We can't prove them wrong and give them hope in the same breath. We can't remind them of the past and inspire them for their future. In short, we can't hear them if we have already judged them. When we are blind with judgment, we are not qualified to help anyone.

Of all the obstacles in our eyes, our judgment may be one of the greatest. Once I decide why a person does what he or she does—once I pass judgment—I must make that person accept my judgment. It is like a doctor who diagnoses without listening to his patient; the "help" will cause more problems. So regardless of our intention, if it doesn't help, it isn't help.

It would be similar to my using a razor to scrape a speck of sawdust out of your eye, even though I am blinded by a stake in my own eye. In the end, we both will be blind.

Proverbs 18:13 says, *"What a shame, what folly, to give advice before listening to the facts!"* (NLT). Our judgments make it impossible to hear what a person is really communicating. The issue becomes more focused on proving our judgment right than on meeting the need of the person. The whole thing becomes about meeting our need instead of the other person's.

Love Is the Key

The very best thing we can do to help others is to help ourselves. We must develop our lives so that we are always motivated by love. We must be able to convey hope, confidence, and trust. We should help people feel loved and safe. We should become models for others to follow rather than experts who fix people.

When people feel that we are trying to fix them, they feel controlled and rejected. They feel like the entire process is about proving them wrong. They feel as if we are imposing our choices on them instead of empowering theirs. When we lead by love, though, people feel inspired and motivated. They see something in us that draws them to us. They seek out our counsel instead of us seeking to counsel them.

We must learn to put our efforts where we are sure they will produce the greatest benefits. (Remember the 80/20 rule?) We do not know if everyone we counsel will get help or if every person we witness to will be saved. We do not know that the time we give to anyone will bear any real fruit. However, we *can* know that our hearts are committed to God. We can know that we are committed to helping others feel the love of God. We can know that every investment we make in our own lives will be worthwhile and fruitful—and will enhance our ability to help others.

Every day there are two commitments we must make. The way we handle these two commitments will determine everything else in our lives. First, will we follow Jesus wholeheartedly today? And, second, will we walk in love? The apostle John said it like this: *"And this is His commandment: that we should believe on the name of His Son Jesus Christ and love one another, as He gave us commandment"* (1 John 3:23 NKJV).

The Greek word for *believe* also means "obey." Believing and obeying are synonymous. The New Testament does not present any concept of believing apart from obeying. The *Amplified Bible* translates it as "to believe in, trust in, adhere to, and rely on." We are not following God, nor are we committed to Him, if we are not committed to walking in love.

Until love motivates us, we cannot trust our intentions. Without love, we will try to fix others instead of lovingly healing them. Until love motivates us, we will be governed by a self-centered agenda that uses ministry as an opportunity to meet our own needs. No matter what the need is in another's life, we will be trying to remove a speck from his eye while a log is stuck in our own eye.

Love is able to see the wrong and still find the good. Love is able to see the weakness and point out the strength. Love is able to be offended by the sin, yet tenderly love the sinner. Love is able to listen patiently and preserve self-worth. Love qualifies you to remove the splinter when the person is ready. And love says the greatest thing that you can do for your neighbor is to pull the log out of your own eye.

So before you seek to help anyone, check with love. Ask yourself, "Am I committed to making this person feel loved? Am I going to approach this individual in a way that makes him or her feel wrong or feel loved?" Until you've answered that question, keep your fingers out of anyone else's eye.

Thirty-six

The Love Factor

If anything will work, love will. If love will not work, nothing will.

Everything Jesus did and modeled in the Gospels demonstrated the love of God. The "love factor" was the missing link in all that the Jews believed about God. They never understood that love was the motivating factor behind all that He said and did. As a result, they arrived at some erroneous concepts of God. They took truth that was given for people's good and turned it into laws that destroyed people. They took the system that was designed to serve people, and they caused people to serve the system. In the end, their beliefs turned the world against God and caused His name to be blasphemed among all the nations.

Paul, on the other hand, said that all instruction is designed to bring people to the place of love—love for God and love for people. *"The purpose of my instruction is that all the Christians there would be filled with love that comes from a pure heart, a clear conscience, and sincere faith"* (1 Timothy 1:5 NLT). Love is the ultimate proof of really knowing God. *"Whoever does not love does not know God, because God is love"* (1 John 4:8 NIV). Love obeys God. It works no wrong toward its neighbor. It actually fulfills the entire law. *"The commandments...are summed up in this one rule: 'Love your neighbor as yourself.' Love does no harm to its neighbor. Therefore love is the fulfillment of the law"* (Romans 13:9–10 NIV).

Even with the mountains of overwhelming Scriptures that place love as the top priority, the church has slipped back into a Pharisaic legalism that views love as a moot point in the Gospel. We are still attempting to do through works, judgment, and control what the law proved could not be done. The law was simply a taskmaster. People spent thousands of years under the law to prove one point: It doesn't work! (See Galatians 3:23–24.) The law has two overwhelming abilities: it makes us feel guilty, and it empowers sin. Nevertheless, our lack of trust in God and His divine principles drives us back to the *"weak and beggarly elements"* of the law. *"But now after you have known God, or rather are known by God, how is it that you turn again to the weak and beggarly elements, to which you desire again to be in bondage?"* (Galatians 4:9 NKJV).

The law imposed control over people; that's all. It never changed a heart or made anyone whole. It never set anyone free from sin or empowered someone to live in righteousness. If it could have done those things, Jesus would not have come and died and given us His grace and righteousness.

The Character of Love

Love does not trust in the power of control. Rather, it trusts in God's principles of acceptance and empowerment. Paul said, *"Love never fails"* (1 Corinthians 13:8 NKJV). The original language indicates that "love never fails to be effective." Spiritual gifts are sometimes effective, but in other situations they can cease to be effective. Love, however, never fails. If anything will work, love will. If love will not work, nothing will. Therefore, Paul advised, *"Make love your aim"* (1 Corinthians 14:1 RSV).

Paul also said that love *"believes all things"* (1 Corinthians 13:7 NKJV). Contrary to carnal thought, love is not naive. Believing all things is not a life of denial. Love is not blind abandonment into the cloudy realms of gullibility. Jesus walked in love, yet He never allowed anyone to take advantage of Him. Love simply believes the best. In his interpretation of Paul's letters to the Corinthians, R. C. H. Lenski said, "Love refuses to yield to suspicious doubt. The flesh is ready to believe all things about a brother and a fellow man in an evil sense. Love does just the opposite."*

In other words, love believes all the best it can. Love sees past the obvious faults right to the most secluded good. People who walk in love are not anxious to judge others; they do not seek validation through judgment. Judgment declares one guilty until innocence is proven. Love, on the other hand, has no need to declare innocence or guilt. Love operates from a personal character that is developed between the believer and God; it does not react to the environment. Love simply relates to people based on the principles of 1 Corinthians 13, whether they deserve it or not.

Living in Love

People who do not have their self-worth established in a meaningful relationship with God need to justify all their actions. If they want to treat you badly, they judge you and find fault. If they want to be kind to you, they judge you good.

The person who lives in judgment does not know how to live free from it. Judgment is his road map for life. They do not know how to trust; therefore, they do not trust God's divine navigation system for life. They do not know how to walk in love. To them, love is something that is given when it is earned or justified. As a result, because they give only conditional love, they cannot receive love unconditionally.

---

* Lenski, R. C. H. *The Interpretation of St. Paul's First and Second Epistles to the Corinthians*. Columbus, Ohio: Lutheran Book Concern, 1935.

Love introduces an unexplainable factor that is unrealized by the person of judgment. You see, love cannot be explained; it can only be experienced. That experience starts when we commit ourselves to a life of love. A process begins that opens our hearts to receive love from both God and people. As we give love to others, we become able to receive love. This life of love frees us from the need to judge. Unconditional love washes away the pain of a mean world.

Love is not just an action; it is a dimension. When we enter this realm, we discover an entirely different world—one that is not subject to the laws of the natural world. It is a realm wherein one can continually experience God, who is love (1 John 4:16 NIV). Faith becomes natural and understandable, for it works through love (Galatians 5:6). Fear has no power. All emotions are ruled by peace and confidence; there is no fear in love (1 John 4:18). It is the realm of the kingdom of God.

This realm is accessible to all believers, yet it is a realm that few will ever enter. The fear of giving up control keeps most believers bound to this world's system—a system that has never given what it promised; a realm where the promises of God fail, faith is a law bound by works, and God appears to be a cruel taskmaster.

Love One Another

Paul said, *"Let all that you do be done in love"* (1 Corinthians 16:14 RSV). Peter said, *"Above all hold unfailing your love for one another, since love covers a multitude of sins"* (1 Peter 4:8 RSV). James said, *"If you really keep the royal law found in Scripture, 'Love your neighbor as yourself,' you are doing right"* (James 2:8 NIV). John said, *"We know that we have passed from death to life, because we love our brothers. Anyone who does not love remains in death"* (1 John 3:14 NIV). Jesus said,

> *"Love the Lord your God with all your heart and with all your soul and with all your mind." This is the first and*

200

greatest commandment. And the second is like it: "Love your neighbor as yourself." All the Law and the Prophets hang on these two commandments.

(Matthew 22:37–40 NIV)

The apostle John wrote, *"This is the message you heard from the beginning: We should love one another"* (1 John 3:11 NIV). There has never been another message from God. Yet corrupt, fearful, and judgmental minds have managed to skirt the issue for six thousand years. We have tried to make this walk be about knowledge. But Paul said, *"Knowledge puffs up, but love builds up"* (1 Corinthians 8:1 NIV).

Because we have made works and judgment the priority, our understanding of God has been inconsistent. Paul said, *"And above all these put on love, which binds everything together in perfect harmony"* (Colossians 3:14 RSV). When love becomes our goal, everything will come together in perfect harmony, and our lives will be filled with the fullness of God. In Ephesians, Paul prayed,

May your roots go down deep into the soil of God's marvelous love. And may you have the power to understand, as all God's people should, how wide, how long, how high, and how deep his love really is. May you experience the love of Christ, though it is so great you will never fully understand it. Then you will be filled with the fullness of life and power that comes from God.

(Ephesians 3:17–19 NLT)

The only antidote for a life of judgment is a life of love. The only real cure for pain is to allow God to love it away. *Know love and know God*—there is no other way to experience the realities that Jesus taught and modeled. If we insist on a life of judgment, maybe we should answer the *why* question like this: "The fact that Jesus loves this brother and gave His life for him is reason enough for me to love him and lay down my life for him."

You will not live a life of love accidentally. Let me say it again: We must make a daily choice to follow Jesus wholeheartedly and to walk in love. That is a choice I make every day. That is my antidote for fear and my propitiation for judgment. So pursue the love-life with all your heart. Make a commitment. Renew yourself daily. You are committed to God only to the degree you are committed to love!

About the Author

~❧❧~

Almost thirty years ago, James Richards found Jesus and answered the call to ministry. His dramatic conversion and passion to help hurting people launched him onto the streets of Huntsville, Alabama. His mission was to reach teenagers and drug abusers.

Before his salvation, James was a professional musician with all the trappings of a worldly lifestyle. More than anything, he was searching for real freedom. Sick of himself and his empty pursuits, he hated all that his life had become. He turned to drugs as a means of escape and relief. Although he was desperate to find God, his emotional outrage made people afraid to tell him about Jesus. He sought help but became more confused and hopeless than before. He heard much religious talk, but not the life-changing Gospel.

Through a miraculous encounter with God, James Richards gave his life to the Lord and was set free from his addictions. His whole life changed! Now, after years of ministry, Dr. Richards still believes there's no one God can't help, and there's no one God doesn't love. He has committed his life to helping people experience that love. If his life is a model for anything, it is that God never quits on anyone.

Dr. Richards—author, teacher, theologian, counselor, and businessman—is president and founder of Impact Ministries, a multifaceted, international ministry committed to helping those whom the church has not yet reached. He is on the cutting edge of what works in today's society. He is president and founder of Impact International School of Ministry, Impact International Fellowship of Ministers, Impact Treatment Center, Impact of Huntsville Church, and Impact International Publications. Thousands have been saved, healed, and delivered every year through his worldwide crusades and pastors' seminars.

With doctorates in theology, human behavior, and alternative medicine, and an honorary doctorate in world evangelism, Dr. Richards is also a certified detox specialist and drug counselor, as well as a trainer for the National Acupuncture Detoxification Association (NADA). His uncompromising yet positive approach to the Gospel strengthens, instructs, and challenges people to new levels of victory, power, and service. Dr. Richards' extensive experience in working with substance abuse, codependency, and other social/emotional issues has led him to pioneer effective, creative, Bible-based approaches to ministry that meet the needs of today's world.

More than anything else, Dr. Richards believes that people need to be made whole by experiencing God's unconditional love. His message is simple, practical, and powerful. His passion is to change the way the world sees God so that they can experience a relationship with Him through Jesus.

He and his wife, Brenda, have five daughters and nine grandchildren and reside in Huntsville, Alabama.

OTHER POWERFUL BOOKS

Distributed through
Whitaker House

Taking the Limits Off God
Dr. James B. Richards
ISBN: 0-92474-800-1
Trade • 96 pages

Supernatural Ministry
Dr. James B. Richards
ISBN: 0-92474-814-1
Trade • 224 pages

Satan Unmasked
Dr. James B. Richards
ISBN: 0-92474-812-5
Trade • 176 pages

OTHER POWERFUL BOOKS

Distributed through
Whitaker House

**Leadership That Builds
People**
Dr. James B. Richards

Vol. I
ISBN: 0-92474-806-0
Workbook • 160 pages

Vol. 2
ISBN: 0-92474-811-7
Workbook • 165 pages

Escape from Codependent Christianity
Dr. James B. Richards
ISBN: 0-92474-810-9
Trade • 214 pages

My Church, My Family
Dr. James B. Richards
ISBN: 0-92474-809-5
Trade • 153 pages

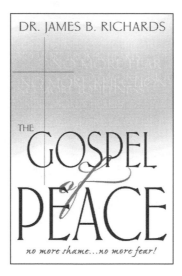